Terrorist Use of Cryptocurrencies

Technical and Organizational Barriers and Future Threats

Cynthia Dion-Schwarz, David Manheim, Patrick B. Johnston

For more information on this publication, visit www.rand.org/t/RR3026

Library of Congress Cataloging-in-Publication Data is available for this publication.

ISBN: 978-1-9774-0234-9

Published by the RAND Corporation, Santa Monica, Calif.

© Copyright 2019 RAND Corporation

RAND® is a registered trademark.

Support RAND
Make a tax-deductible charitable contribution at
www.rand.org/giving/contribute

www.rand.org

Preface

This report examines the possibility of more-widespread adoption of cryptocurrency by terrorist groups by considering both the needs of such groups and the advantages and disadvantages of the cryptocurrency technologies available to them.

This research should be of interest to a wide variety of stakeholders, including policymakers concerned with counterterrorism, those making decisions about international regulation and harmonization, and people who work with and invest in cryptocurrencies.

The research was conducted within the International Security and Defense Policy Center of the RAND National Security Research Division (NSRD). NSRD conducts research and analysis for the Office of the Secretary of Defense, the Joint Staff, the Unified Combatant Commands, the defense agencies, the Navy, the Marine Corps, the U.S. Coast Guard, the U.S. Intelligence Community, allied foreign governments, and foundations. This research was funded through a generous grant from a private foundation.

For more information on the RAND International Security and Defense Policy Center, see www.rand.org/nsrd/ndri/centers/isdp or contact the director (contact information is provided on the webpage).

Contents

Tables

Summary

Given the key role of funding in supporting terrorist operations, counterterrorism efforts—in particular, the subfield of counterterrorism finance (CTF)—often focus on tracking the flow of money through bank accounts and preventing financial transactions that might be used to support attacks and other terrorist activities. However, the success of CTF strategies in reducing terrorist access to fiat (i.e., government-issued) currencies has raised concerns that terrorist organizations might increase their use of such digital cryptocurrencies as Bitcoin to support their activities.

Bitcoin is both a protocol for securely storing and transmitting tokens (virtual coins) and the name of the unit of value in the system. Bitcoin revolves around a public ledger called the *blockchain*, which is maintained by an online peer-to-peer network that tracks transactions and maintains a complete history of verified transactions. Media reports have outlined the notion that some, or even many, terrorist organizations have unlimited, untraceable sources of digital money, such as Bitcoin, which will be used to undermine the successes of CTF.[1] Policymakers also have raised concerns about terrorist use of digital currencies.[2]

---

[1] Heather Nauert, "ISIS Parks Its Cash in Bitcoin, Experts Say," Fox News, November 2011; Ian McKendry, "ISIL May Be Using Bitcoin, Fincen's Calvery Says," *American Banker*, November 16, 2015; Resty Woro Yuniar, "Bitcoin, PayPal Used to Finance Terrorism, Indonesian Agency Says," *Wall Street Journal*, January 10, 2017.

[2] U.S. House of Representatives, Financial Innovation and Defense Act, H.R. 4752, January 20, 2018.

However, the challenge posed by cryptocurrencies extends beyond Bitcoin. Many new cryptocurrencies have emerged in the past few years, including such alternative currencies (altcoins) as Omni Layer (MasterCoin), BlackCoin, and Monero, which are touted as more private and secure than Bitcoin. Zcash is another cryptocurrency that offers a higher degree of privacy and provides the potential ability to use and transfer currency offline, which could make it difficult for law enforcement to trace illicit transactions. Other cryptocurrencies have been proposed, including Hawk, which would allow fully private contracts and transactions on the Ethereum blockchain. Like Bitcoin, the Ethereum blockchain is a distributed computing platform and operating system.

There is thus a great need to understand the full potential for terrorist use of cryptocurrencies, including options for identifying and tracking their use, the sophistication and technological capability of terrorist groups, and the potential for such use to increase in the future, given expected technological developments.

This report focuses on two key questions. First, we aim to understand whether terrorist groups are currently using cryptocurrencies to support their activities and, if not, why they are not using such currencies. Second, we want to understand what properties of new and future cryptocurrencies, such as the potential for improved anonymity and high-volume transactions, would make them more viable for terrorist use—that is, more difficult for law enforcement to identify and track. To answer these questions, the research team conducted an extensive literature review of scholarly works and news reports on terrorist organizations, terrorism finance and economics, and cryptocurrencies. In addition, the team interviewed current and former members of the intelligence community and law enforcement engaged in CTF. The team used these data to identify several major areas in which terrorist groups require financing, whether for supporting major attacks or providing for day-to-day operations. These data also were analyzed to identify similarities and differences among major terrorist groups with respect to their uses of finance for their activities. Finally, the properties (i.e., strengths and weaknesses) of major and emerging cryptocurrencies were identified and compared with terrorist finance requirements.

How Are Terrorist Groups Currently Using Cryptocurrencies?

In order to understand the potential for terrorist use of cryptocurrencies, it is useful first to consider the broader question of how terrorist organizations use money and then to identify needs and opportunities for such use. We examine terrorist organizations' use of money in three parts: *receipt*, *management*, and *spending*. In particular, we identified several subcategories for terrorist use of money, which we outline in Table S.1.

All of these categories pose significant challenges to terrorist organizations' use of cryptocurrencies: Large receipted sums are difficult to manage or spend anonymously, and cryptocurrencies still require infrastructure to manage and spend. We see little current evidence of the adoption of cryptocurrencies by terrorist organizations or the motivation to do so, but that very well might change as countermeasures shut off funding and as the cryptocurrency technology changes.

Potential for Cryptocurrencies to Facilitate Terrorist Finance Operations

Whether and how terrorist organizations would use a cryptocurrency system depends on the available technology and its properties, as well as on the organization's needs and capabilities. Newer cryptocurrencies might emerge with properties that terrorist organizations find

Table S.1
Terrorist Organization Financial Activities

Activity Name	Components of Activity in Finance
Fundraising	Receipt of support from donors, especially cash support
Illegal drug and arms trafficking	Income source
Remittance and transfer of funds	Sending or receiving funds to support organizational activities
Attack funding	Direct purchase of materiel to support terrorist attacks and financial support of attack operations
Operational funding	Use of funds to support the terrorist organization on a day-to-day basis, including general security, communications, and management

more attractive than those of currently available cryptocurrencies. For instance, if a future cryptocurrency provides better anonymity than Bitcoin for large-sum transactions and is more widely adopted than Zcash, then terrorist organizations might be willing to employ that currency for specific activities. Thus, it is important to look at individual terrorist groups to analyze what they would need from cryptocurrencies and compare those needs with the properties of available cryptocurrencies.

We considered a set of useful examples: specifically, al Qaeda and affiliates, the Islamic State of Iraq and Syria (ISIS),[3] Hezbollah, narcoterrorist organizations, and lone-wolf attackers. Although these groups differ in their goals, their need for anonymous, secure, and ready streams of funding make cryptocurrencies of some potential value to them. For these groups, we examined five financial activities (fundraising, illegal drug and arms trafficking, remittance and transfer of funds, attack funding, and operational funding) and evaluated the importance of cryptocurrency properties in facilitating these activities. These properties are anonymity, usability, security, acceptance, reliability, and volume. By *anonymity*, we mean the ability to hide and protect the identity of the user. *Usability* refers to the ease with which the user can conduct transactions and manage his or her own currency. *Security* refers to the degree to which the cryptocurrency infrastructure secures the confidentiality, integrity, and accuracy of transactions and user accounts. By *acceptance*, we mean the degree to which the currency is accepted by a user community as well as the size of the community of users. *Reliability* refers to the speed and availability of transactions, as viewed by users. Finally, *volume* refers to the time-averaged aggregate size of transactions in the cryptocurrency infrastructure.

No cryptocurrency uniformly offers these features to terrorist organizations; in particular, security of current cryptocurrencies is

---

3   The organization's name transliterates from Arabic as al-Dawlah al-Islamiyah fi al-'Iraq wa al-Sham (abbreviated as Da'ish or DAESH). In the West, it is commonly referred to as the Islamic State of Iraq and the Levant (ISIL), the Islamic State of Iraq and Syria, the Islamic State of Iraq and the Sham (both abbreviated as ISIS), or simply as the Islamic State (IS). Arguments abound as to which is the most accurate translation, but here we refer to the group as ISIS.

probably inadequate for terrorist organization needs. Our assessment is shown in Table S.2. Each box is scored and shaded as of "critical importance" (gray), "moderate importance" (light gray), or "lesser importance" (white).

Security in the cryptocurrency infrastructure is of moderate to high importance for terrorist organizations, yet current cryptocurrencies are vulnerable to a variety of cyberattacks. Even newer currencies that are thought to improve security are subject to significant scrutiny, and new security vulnerabilities are discovered over time.

When we consider all our assessments together, including other important properties, such as reliability and volume of the cryptocurrency market, we find that no current cryptocurrency can address all of the terrorist organizations' financial needs. However, we note that such cryptocurrencies as Bitcoin, particularly with improved usability, could be appealing to use in fundraising, and some evidence is emerging that terrorist organizations might be using cryptocurrencies for this purpose. Thus, we conclude that current cryptocurrencies generally are not well matched with the totality of features that would be needed by and desirable to the terrorist groups examined but might be employed for selected financial activities.

Table S.2
Assessment of Terrorist Finance Activities with Respect to Cryptocurrency Properties

	Fundraising	Illegal Drug and Arms Trafficking	Remittance and Transfer	Attack Funding	Operational Funding
Anonymity	Moderate importance	Critical importance	Moderate importance	Critical importance	Lesser importance
Usability	Critical importance	Lesser importance	Lesser importance	Lesser importance	Lesser importance
Security	Moderate importance	Critical importance	Critical importance	Critical importance	Critical importance
Acceptance	Lesser importance	Lesser importance	Lesser importance	Moderate importance	Moderate importance
Reliability	Lesser importance	Moderate importance	Critical importance	Critical importance	Moderate importance
Volume	Moderate importance	Lesser importance	Critical importance	Lesser importance	Critical importance

What Properties of Future Cryptocurrencies Would Make Them More Viable for Terrorist Use?

The utility of cryptocurrencies in the future as both terrorist methods and the cryptocurrencies themselves develop is unclear. Nonetheless, several recent advances in cryptocurrencies will facilitate their use by the most sophisticated groups that threaten terrorism against Western countries, and the use of cryptocurrencies will be especially enabling for actors that already engage in transnational fundraising and criminal activities. Our research shows that, should a single cryptocurrency emerge that provides widespread adoption, better anonymity, improved security, and that is subject to lax or inconsistent regulation, then the potential utility of this cryptocurrency, as well as the potential for its use by terrorist organizations, would increase. Even if no such currency emerges, there will be some use by terrorist groups, but the extent of that use will depend on the currency's viability. In particular, factors that tend to discourage use include continued instability and infighting in the cryptocurrency community, cooperation between international law enforcement and the intelligence community, and developments in regulation and enforcement.

Conclusion

Concerns about the use of cryptocurrency to enable terrorist activities have yet to manifest, but coming improvements in cryptocurrency technologies will likely have a significant long-term effect on terrorism finance. The speed at which these technologies are adopted, and the details of which technologies are used and how they are deployed, are critical uncertainties that have important operational impacts. This analysis suggests that regulation and oversight of cryptocurrencies, along with international cooperation between law enforcement and the intelligence community, would be important steps to prevent terrorist organizations from using cryptocurrencies to support their activities.

Acknowledgments

The authors wish to thank Matt Levine of the Washington Institute and Allison Ickovic at the U.S. Department of Justice for their insight and suggestions, as well as Zooko Wilcox-Hearn for details and insight into Zcash. We also thank our reviewers, Angela O'Mahony and Akhil Shah, who provided valuable insights and greatly strengthened the manuscript.

Although we received help and insights from those acknowledged, it does not necessarily imply that they concur with the views expressed in this report. Any errors are the responsibility of the authors alone.

Abbreviations

9/11	September 11, 2001, terrorist attacks
AQI	al Qaeda in Iraq
CTF	counterterrorism finance
DDoS	distributed denial of service
FATF	Financial Action Task Force
IP	internet protocol
ISIS	Islamic State of Iraq and Syria
NGO	nongovernmental organization

CHAPTER ONE

Introduction

Terrorists require significant funding to carry out attacks and other activities. Indeed, there is reason to believe that, if terrorist groups were better funded overall, there might be more-frequent, more-successful, and larger attacks.[1] There are several reasons that support this belief. First, more funds for operations would presumably lead to increased funding for the structures that enable these attacks, which include recruiting and training attackers and inspiring potential lone wolves. Second, groups facing less monetary pressure (i.e., those that are better funded) also might be more willing to take risks, such as larger or riskier attacks.[2] Lastly, and perhaps more contentiously, increased funds can be used directly for additional and larger attacks. It might be difficult to directly link increased funds to terrorist attacks, although in specific documented cases, "the literature often describes shortages of cash as a problem for terrorist operations."[3] It is therefore plausible that the relative lack of attacks, and especially the lack of higher-cost large attacks, is partly because of overall funding constraints.

Since the September 11, 2001, terrorist attacks (9/11), law enforcement agencies have developed and implemented several successful approaches for preventing the flow of fiat (i.e., government-issued) cur-

[1] Arabinda Acharya, *Targeting Terrorist Financing: International Cooperation and New Regimes*, New York: Routledge, 2009.

[2] Jacob N. Shapiro, "Terrorist Decision-Making: Insights from Economics and Political Science," *Perspectives on Terrorism*, Vol. 6, No. 4–5, 2012.

[3] Emilie Oftedal, *The Financing of Jihadi Terrorist Cells in Europe*, Norway: Forsvarets Forskningsinstitutt, January 6, 2015.

rencies to terrorist groups. In particular, as intelligence and counterterrorism agencies have identified finance strategies employed by terrorist organizations, they have been able to curtail terrorist fundraising.[4]

However, the success of counterterrorism finance (CTF) strategies in reducing terrorist access to fiat currencies has raised concerns that terrorist organizations might increase their use of such digital cryptocurrencies as Bitcoin to support their activities.[5] Bitcoin is both a protocol for securely storing and transmitting tokens (virtual coins) and the name of the unit of value in the system. Bitcoin revolves around a public ledger called the *blockchain*, which is maintained by an online distributed network of computers that track transactions and maintain a complete history of verified transactions. Any user of the system can participate in all aspects of its operations, including all transactions, and no single participant has control. To support anonymity and transaction ownership, Bitcoin transaction participants are identified by a unique string of random numbers rather than by a name or other personal information.

Furthermore, the challenge posed by cryptocurrencies extends beyond Bitcoin. Many new cryptocurrencies have emerged, all with differing properties tailored for different audiences, some of which might align with terrorists' needs. These include such other alternative currencies ("altcoins") as Omni Layer (MasterCoin), BlackCoin, and Monero, which are touted as more private and secure than Bitcoin and therefore are seemingly tailor-made for illicit activities.[6] Another cryptocurrency is Zcash, which uses transactions that are not identified by any owner, thereby offering a higher degree of privacy. Zcash also offers a higher degree of privacy, which could make it even more difficult for law enforcement to trace illicit transactions and could be extended to

---

4   For instance, U.S. banks are required to verify the identities of account holders (e.g., "know your customer") and report large or suspicious patterns of transactions.

5   Heather Nauert, "ISIS Parks Its Cash in Bitcoin, Experts Say," Fox News, November 2011; Ian McKendry, "ISIL May Be Using Bitcoin, Fincen's Calvery Says," *American Banker*, November 16, 2015; Resty Woro Yuniar, "Bitcoin, PayPal Used to Finance Terrorism, Indonesian Agency Says," *Wall Street Journal*, January 10, 2017.

6   See "Omni Layer," homepage, undated; "BlackCoin," homepage, undated; and "Monero. How," homepage, undated.

allow offline use and transfer of the currency. Other types of cryptocurrencies have been proposed, including Hawk, which aims to allow fully private contracts and transactions on the Ethereum blockchain. Like Bitcoin, the Ethereum blockchain is a distributed computing platform and operating system.

Increased use of cryptocurrencies by terrorists could undermine the successes of CTF. Although terrorist organizations have sometimes been reluctant to adopt new methods when old methods are effective, CTF pressures can create incentives for terrorists to innovate, as we have seen in other domains.[7] We might expect terrorist groups to expand their use of cryptocurrencies in cases where their access to alternative financial systems is limited, or where cryptocurrency provides significant benefits over alternatives.

Some research has been conducted on the use of cryptocurrencies by criminals and terrorist organizations, but such research has largely focused on Bitcoin and other first-generation cryptocurrencies (with some notable exceptions).[8] Policymakers also have focused more attention on terrorists' potential use of digital currencies, including Bitcoin. For example, in January 2018, a bill was introduced in Congress to ask the U.S. Treasury Department to "prioritize the investigation of terrorist and illicit use of new financial technology, including digital curren-

---

[7] Shapiro, 2012; Seth G. Jones and Patrick B. Johnston, "The Future of Insurgency," *Studies in Conflict and Terrorism*, Vol. 36, No. 1, 2013.

[8] For research on the use of cryptocurrencies by criminals, see Steven David Brown "Cryptocurrency and Criminality: The Bitcoin Opportunity," *Police Journal: Theory, Practice and Principles*, Vol. 89, No. 4, December 2016. For cryptocurrency use by terrorist organizations, see Anaïs Carmona, "The Bitcoin: The Currency of the Future, Fuel of Terror," in Misty Blowers, ed., *Evolution of Cyber Technologies and Operations to 2035*, Switzerland: Springer International Publishing, 2015; Alan Brill and Lonnie Keene, "Cryptocurrencies: The Next Generation of Terrorist Financing?" *Defence Against Terrorism Review*, Vol. 6, No. 1, 2014; and Zachary K. Goldman, Ellie Maruyama, Elizabeth Rosenberg, Edoardo Saravalle, and Julia Solomon-Strauss, *Terrorist Use of Virtual Currencies: Containing the Potential Threat*, Washington, D.C.: Center for a New American Security, May 2017. For research on the use of Bitcoin and other first-generation technologies, see Diana Mergenovna Sat, Grigory Olegovich Krylov, Kirill Evgenyevich Bezverbnyi, Alexander Borisovich Kasatkin, and Ivan Aleksandrovich Kornev, "Investigation of Money Laundering Methods Through Cryptocurrency," *Journal of Theoretical and Applied Information Technology*, Vol. 83, No. 2, 2016, p. 244.

cies," among other provisions.[9] There is thus a great need to understand the full potential for terrorist use of cryptocurrencies, including options for identifying and tracking their use, the sophistication and technological capability of terrorist groups, and the potential for such use to increase in the future, given expected technological developments.

Focus of This Report

This report focuses on two key questions. First, we aim to understand whether terrorist groups are currently using cryptocurrencies to support their activities and, if not, why they are not using such currencies. Second, we want to understand what properties of new and future cryptocurrencies, such as the potential for improved anonymity and high-volume transactions, would make them more viable for terrorist use—that is, more difficult for law enforcement to identify and track.

Despite little indication that cryptocurrencies are currently a significant factor in terrorist finance, we expect that several recent advances in cryptocurrencies will facilitate their use by the most sophisticated groups that threaten terrorism against Western countries, and that the use of cryptocurrencies will be especially enabling for actors that already engage in transnational fundraising and criminal activities.

Methodology

The research team conducted an extensive literature review of scholarly works and news reports on terrorist organizations, terrorism finance and economics, and cryptocurrencies. In addition, the team interviewed current and former members of the intelligence community and law enforcement engaged in CTF. The team used these data to identify several major areas in which terrorist groups require financing, whether for supporting major attacks or providing for day-to-day

9   U.S. House of Representatives, Financial Innovation and Defense Act, H.R. 4752, January 20, 2018.

operations. These data also were analyzed to identify similarities and differences among major terrorist groups with respect to their uses of finance for their activities. Finally, the properties (i.e., strengths and weaknesses) of major and emerging cryptocurrencies were identified and compared with terrorist finance requirements.

Organization of This Report

Chapter Two discusses how terrorist organizations use money and identifies needs and opportunities for such use, while Chapter Three describes the limitations of current cryptocurrency systems. Chapter Four discusses several technical attacks that could be used to thwart the use of cryptocurrencies by terrorist organizations. Chapter Five identifies factors that can increase or decrease the future viability of cryptocurrencies for terrorist use, and Chapter Six presents our conclusions. The appendix provides a short primer on cryptocurrencies.

CHAPTER TWO

How Terrorist Groups Use Money

In order to understand the potential for terrorist use of cryptocurrencies, it is useful first to consider the broader question of how terrorist organizations use money and identify needs and opportunities for such use. Based on conceptual models used in previous research,[1] we consider three parts of terrorist organizations' use of money: receipt, management, and spending. For each, we discuss variation among different groups, outline some current pressures, and note whether there are significant funding constraints that might prompt the use of alternative methods, such as cryptocurrency (e.g., because of law enforcement pressure).

This analysis implies a potentially troubling avenue for cryptocurrency use in the short term: the use of cryptocurrency to help fund attacks more easily than is done today with fiat currencies. Although terrorist use of darknet markets for acquiring weapons is a troubling possibility, it is unlikely that cryptocurrency would be used to directly purchase equipment for an attack.[2] Instead, attackers in Western countries could convert funds in cryptocurrency accounts into fiat cur-

---

[1] Jayesh D'Souza, *Terrorist Financing, Money Laundering, and Tax Evasion: Examining the Performance of Financial Intelligence Units*, New York: CRC Press, Taylor and Francis Group, 2012, especially chapters 1–4; Colin P. Clarke, *Terrorism, Inc.: The Financing of Terrorism, Insurgency, and Irregular Warfare*, Santa Barbara, Calif.: Praeger Security International, 2015; and Michael Freeman and Moyara Ruehsen, "Terrorism Financing Methods: An Overview," *Perspectives on Terrorism*, Vol. 7, No. 4, August 2013.

[2] Giacomo Persi Paoli, Judith Aldridge, Nathan Ryan, and Richard Warnes, *Behind the Curtain: The Illicit Trade of Firearms, Explosives and Ammunition on the Dark Web*, Santa Monica, Calif.: RAND Corporation, RR-2091-PACCS, 2017.

rencies, drawing on either funds provided by a central organization or crowdfunding, which would be a convenient way for the terrorist organization to supply funding to the attacker. Of course, many cryptocurrency exchanges are subject to banking regulations for suspicious activities, so it may still be difficult to withdraw large amounts of cash. Nonetheless, should a poorly regulated cryptocurrency emerge, it would provide an attractive avenue for terrorist organizational transactions, such as accepting donations or financing activities.

Receipt

Oftedal notes that the most-common sources of terrorist funding are state sponsorship, charitable or personal donations, illegal activities (including drug trafficking and other smuggling and fraud, extortion, and petty crime), and legal sources (such as salaried employment, legitimate businesses, and personal or credit-based loans).[3] A group's choice of source varies greatly according to availability and group preferences and may evolve over time. The success of intelligence and law enforcement agencies in constraining the ability of terrorist groups to raise money can lead terrorist organizations to search for alternative fundraising methods, which in turn leads authorities to develop new countermeasures.

For instance, as outlined by Johnston and colleagues, the Islamic State of Iraq and Syria (ISIS)[4] previously generated almost all of its funding from its control of territory.[5] Funding sources included taxa-

---

3   Oftedal, 2015.

4   The organization's name transliterates from Arabic as al-Dawlah al-Islamiyah fi al-'Iraq wa al-Sham (abbreviated as Da'ish or DAESH). In the West, it is commonly referred to as the Islamic State of Iraq and the Levant (ISIL), the Islamic State of Iraq and Syria, the Islamic State of Iraq and the Sham (both abbreviated as ISIS), or simply as the Islamic State (IS). Arguments abound as to which is the most accurate translation, but here we refer to the group as ISIS.

5   Patrick B. Johnston, Jacob N. Shapiro, Howard J. Shatz, Benjamin Bahney, Danielle F. Jung, Patrick K. Ryan, and Jonathan Wallace, *Foundations of the Islamic State: Management, Money, and Terror in Iraq, 2005–2010*, Santa Monica, Calif.: RAND Corporation,

tion, sale of natural resources (especially oil), appropriation of government assets in ISIS-controlled territory, and so-called "spoils" and looting (e.g., historical artifacts, cars, and anything else confiscated). ISIS engaged in little fundraising or illegal fundraising activities outside its territory. More recently, however, ISIS (mimicking al Qaeda) has shifted toward illegal fundraising activities and home-grown sources of funding, whereas Hezbollah increasingly relies on Iranian funding because its illegal revenue sources (such as drug smuggling) have been choked off.[6]

Cryptocurrencies might aid terrorists in the receipt of funding through various means. For example, although public support for these groups represents a minority view throughout much of the Muslim world, it is not inconsequential. Thus, if Sunni supporters are not donating as much to terrorist groups as they did in the past because of an increase in the legal and financial risks involved in doing so, it is plausible that a sufficiently robust, secure, and anonymous cryptocurrency could re-enable donations as a significant source of terrorist financing. Supporters might donate their own cryptocurrencies or use cryptocurrencies to transfer funds through broker intermediaries. Over the past decade, the dismantling of finance networks supporting al Qaeda has vastly reduced its funding. However, some support might have shifted to alternative methods of funding jihad, either through supporting ISIS or finding other outlets. The total amount of such donations to specific organizations is not fixed: Even if funding from so-called "deep-pocket donors" is somewhat fixed, the distribution of these funds varies over time. An economic approach to the question of how much support is given to terrorist groups would show that a giver's willingness to donate can be reduced by an increase in the perceived level of risk to the giver. Conversely, this willingness can increase according to the perceived impact of the funds.[7]

RR-1192-DARPA, 2016; Charlie Winter and Colin P. Clarke, "Is ISIS Breaking Apart? What Its Media Operations Suggest," *Foreign Affairs*, January 31, 2017.

[6] Matthew Levitt, "Hezbollah's Transnational Organized Crime," The Washington Institute for Near East Policy, April 21, 2016.

[7] The authors are grateful to our RAND colleague Eric Larsen for this insight.

The sale of illegal goods and drug trafficking also may be critically assisted by cryptocurrencies, and the darknet markets that play a significant role in cryptocurrency economies already make this possibility plausible. It is currently unlikely that some types of trafficking of concern (such as in antiquities and weapons) would be conducted easily on these forums. Other trafficking, especially for drugs, is already occurring extensively on darknet markets, but it is unclear whether terrorist groups are involved, in part because these markets are not yet used heavily in the areas of the world where terrorist groups engage in drug trafficking.

Management and Transfer

Once funds are generated, terrorist organizations must manage their money. If the money received is not yet under the direct control of the terrorist organization or if it cannot be transferred because of operational security concerns, money laundering and other transfer mechanisms may be used. This is more critical for groups that rely on external funding and less critical for primarily territorial groups, such as ISIS, which have few external sources of funds, and for smaller groups or lone-wolf attackers that self-fund. Hezbollah, which relies more heavily on state sponsorship, has access to banking systems in Iran and Libya, while al Qaeda and affiliates generally must use other methods.

As noted earlier, Western governments have significantly increased the enforcement of anti–money laundering regulations since 9/11. In addition to affecting fundraising, this increased enforcement has significantly reduced the ability of terrorist groups to rely on formal banking, especially money transfer services, an expansive category that can include digital transfers, prepaid instruments, and mobile payment systems.[8] These regulations now directly target terrorist use of nongovernmental organizations (NGOs) and charities. Informal transfer systems

---

8   Code of Federal Regulations, Title 31, Money and Finance; Treasury; Subtitle B, Regulations Relating to Money and Finance; Subchapter X, Financial Crimes Enforcement Network, Department of the Treasury; Parts 1010, 1021, and 1022, Bank Secrecy Act Regulations; Definitions and Other Regulations Relating to Money Services Businesses.

and false trade invoicing have been targeted because of their use by al Qaeda, Hezbollah, and other groups.[9]

Freeman and Reuhsen provide a useful list of the ways in which terrorist organizations transfer money, including "cash couriers, informal transfer systems (e.g., hawala), money service businesses, formal banking, false trade invoicing, and high value commodities."[10] Lindholm and Realuyo add NGOs and charities; prepaid instruments; mobile payments; and virtual payments, such as cryptocurrencies.[11] The attributes that Lindholm and Realuyo list as important considerations for money transfer methods apply to cryptocurrencies. These are anonymity, usability, security, acceptance, reliability, and volume. We will discuss these considerations further in Chapter Three, but they also are worth considering as aspects of management and transfer.

Although all of these attributes are important to terrorist organizations, transaction volume is particularly critical at present because, while the total daily transaction volume for Bitcoin is more than $1 billion, most transactions occur within a few specific countries and are either internal funds transfers or settlements between known parties. Large transactions may therefore be difficult—and noticeable. This creates a potential trade-off for Bitcoin users between volume, cost, risk, and speed. Large fund transfers via Bitcoin that occur quickly would require the purchase of enough bitcoin to be noticeable by authorities, creating risk, and would change market prices, increasing costs. Other cryptocurrencies can offer more anonymity but are orders of magnitude smaller in volume compared with Bitcoin. The solution to this problem would be to move funds in smaller amounts incrementally, slowing the process and creating risks because of both the volatil-

9 Juan C. Zarate, "Learning Curve," in *Treasury's War: The Unleashing of a New Era of Financial Warfare*, New York: PublicAffairs, Perseus Book Group, 2013, pp. 357–382.

10 Freeman and Ruehsen, 2013.

11 Danielle Camner Lindholm and Celina B. Realuyo, "Threat Finance: A Critical Enabler for Illicit Networks," in Michael Miklaucic and Jacqueline Brewer, eds., *Convergence: Illicit Networks and National Security in the Age of Globalization*, Washington, D.C.: National Defense University Press, April 2013, pp. 111–130.

ity of the currency and exchange rates and the potential for discovery by authorities.

In addition, there are significant hurdles to the usability (that is, convenience and simplicity) of cryptocurrencies for transferring funds. Use of cryptocurrency has become easier, but it still requires a significant level of technological sophistication, especially if transactions are done securely and without compromising anonymity. The eventual transfer of money to the less developed regions in which terrorist groups operate is also challenging, as we discuss further below.

Management of funds by terrorist organizations also can be challenging with regard to cryptocurrency. As noted by the Financial Action Task Force (FATF), large organizations rely on relatively sophisticated financial infrastructure with multiple levels of management, reporting and accounting, and financial planning.[12] Johnston and colleagues explain that terrorist organizations under attack, like ISIS, must pay attention to the robustness of their financial systems to limit or prevent losses of personnel, sites, or records.[13] Cryptocurrencies may not be well suited to this type of robustness, because loss of technological expertise or loss of access to the cryptographic keys could lead to a complete loss of the funds. Thus, it seems unlikely that these groups would want to maintain balances or manage their money via cryptocurrency in the near term, as discussed in Baron et al.[14]

Spending

Finally, terrorist groups spend the funds they have collected. For our purposes, we can differentiate between operating costs and costs to

12 FATF, *Emerging Terrorist Financing Risks*, Paris: Financial Action Task Force and the Organisation for Economic Co-operation and Development, October 2015.

13 Johnston et al., 2016.

14 Joshua Baron, Angela O'Mahony, David Manheim, and Cynthia Dion-Schwarz, *National Security Implications of Virtual Currencies: Examining the Potential for Non-state Actor Deployment*, Santa Monica, Calif.: RAND Corporation, RR-1231-OSD, 2015.

produce violence. Both categories typically are funded by the same mechanisms.

Different terrorist groups will budget differently based on their needs and goals, and the operations to track and disrupt the activities of such groups will have different effects, depending on the choices made. It is difficult to separate licit operations and expenses, such as salaries and social services, from clearly illicit spending, such as terrorism recruitment and training, because of the lack of information about and the close relationship between these activities, and especially because the legitimate activities create incentives and inducements to illegal actions.[15] For example, operating costs, such as propaganda, recruitment, salaries, and social services, indirectly contribute to an organization's ability to produce violence, making such activities a useful target for CTF. Spending by terrorist groups is more difficult now than in the past, largely because of CTF operations, which potentially makes alternatives like cryptocurrency more tempting for these groups.

Most terrorist groups are currently constrained in their ability to use cryptocurrency because of the limited acceptability and usability of these currencies in the regions in which terrorist groups operate. Even if a group receives and manages these funds, they cannot easily be used to pay for expenses where vendors and members expect cash, either in stable currencies like dollars and euros, or in local currencies. For instance, few Bitcoin ATMs exist in the Middle East, making it difficult to exchange bitcoins for fiat currencies. Bitcoin ATMs tend to be more prevalent in Europe and the United States, where local banking and currency laws provide something of a deterrent to illicit use.

The potential critical exception is direct operational costs for overseas attacks by affiliates of the al Qaeda network or independent cells like those inspired by ISIS, which are hard to disrupt via CTF. Most cells in Europe and North America appear to be self-financed, and many centrally directed cells are partially self-financed as well.[16] This may be because most attacks have been relatively cheap: The sig-

---

15 Eli Berman, *Radical, Religious, and Violent: The New Economics of Terrorism*, Cambridge, Mass.: MIT Press, 2009.

16 Oftedal, 2015.

nificant majority of attacks have cost less than $10,000, the U.S. bank reporting threshold for suspicious activities.[17]

Terrorist Organizations' Current and Future Needs for Cryptocurrency

The question of whether and how terrorist organizations would use a cryptocurrency system depends on the available technology and its properties, as well as the groups' needs and capabilities. Newer cryptocurrencies may emerge with properties that terrorist organizations find more attractive than those of currently available cryptocurrencies. For instance, if a future cryptocurrency provides better anonymity than Bitcoin for large-sum transactions and is more widely adopted than Zcash, then terrorist organizations might be willing to employ that currency for specific activities. Thus, it is important to look at individual terrorist groups to analyze what they would need from cryptocurrencies and compare those needs with the properties of available cryptocurrencies.

In our analysis, we identified five categories of terrorist organization finance activities: fundraising, illegal drug/arms trafficking, remittance/transfer, attack funding, and operational funding:

- Fundraising is required by terrorist organizations to support all other activities, including purchase of weapons, payrolls, supporting attacks, and other operational activities. As noted earlier, fundraising can have a variety of sources, including nation-states, charities, and individual donors.

- Illegal drug and arms trafficking can be a source of income to support the terrorist organization.

- Remittance and transfer activities are required by terrorist organizations to support the cash needs of their members and associates, including payroll and operational or other support expenses.

---

17 Oftedal, 2015.

- Attack funding activities support terrorist attacks and can include weapons purchases or other operational expenses.
- Operational activities support general security, communications, and management of the organization and its finances.

We summarize these financial activities in Table 2.1.

Using the structure described earlier in this chapter to categorize terrorist groups' use of funds (receipt, management and transfer, spending), we considered what is known about how funds are used by specific organizations. In this brief review, we look at al Qaeda and its affiliates, ISIS, Hezbollah, narcoterrorist organizations, and lone-wolf attackers. These entities were chosen for their representative differences. For each group, we review both typical and historical funding mechanisms that may encourage changes and the ways in which some of the pressures—such as increasing successful counterterrorism actions or the loss of income sources—may be promoting those changes.[18]

Table 2.1
Terrorist Organization Financial Activities

Activity Name	Components of Activity in Finance
Fundraising	Receipt of support from donors, especially cash support
Illegal drug and arms trafficking	Income source
Remittance and transfer of funds	Sending or receiving funds to support organizational activities
Attack funding	Direct purchase of materiel to support terrorist attacks and financial support of attack operations
Operational funding	Use of funds to support the terrorist organization on a day-to-day basis, including general security, communications, and management

---

[18] Of course, these groups are not static and, as Zarate notes, "Terrorist financing for the broader Sunni violent extremist movement . . . was reliant . . . on key donors and donations." And the financing is likely to be ongoing, "a generational struggle . . . with supporters of terrorist causes in the Arabian Gulf" (Zarate, 2013, p. 83). We expect new groups, and similar groups that are omitted from this analysis, to pursue funding in similar ways.

With the continued focus on CTF, we expect the financing strategies of terrorist groups to become more diverse in both expected and surprising ways in terms of their sources and uses of funds. For each example, we will describe specific areas of concern for the use of cryptocurrency and more-general causes and indications of pressure on group finances.

The history of repeated adaptations and the evolution of terrorist groups provide exemplars of how funding changes occur via adaptation and innovation. Generally, the recent successes in CTF have led to new terrorist sources of funds that are less vulnerable to interception. Because of the availability of viable solutions, terrorist organizations may be less likely to adopt new technologies. At the same time, new countermeasures that cut off funding sources would promote the use of innovations in terrorists' funding streams, perhaps including the adoption of cryptocurrencies. Put another way, we see little current evidence of the adoption of cryptocurrencies by terrorist organizations or the motivation to do so, but that might change as countermeasures shut off funding and as the cryptocurrency technology changes.

Al Qaeda

Before the post-9/11 crackdown on al Qaeda, the organization was heavily funded by donations and Islamic charitable funds (primarily Zakat, but also Sadaqah).[19] Much of this funding was done through such informal but legal channels as the hawala network; formal channels, including traditional banks; and illegal but hard-to-trace movements of cash. The U.S. government was successful in tracing funds across these different channels and bringing criminal charges against those that were involved in terrorist finance. This effort was largely successful in cutting off funds by both dissuading participants and shutting down many of the channels involved.

However, the extent to which Zakat fundraising for al Qaeda came from individuals intending to support terrorism or from funds misdi-

---

[19] *Zakat* is an obligatory annual payment made under Islamic law that is used for charitable and religious purposes, while *Sadaqah* is a voluntary contribution made under Islamic law that is used for the same purposes.

rected from legitimate charities is unclear. Some funding was clearly from those intending to promote terrorism: "Donors . . . were often not just passive contributors, but demanding investors in a cause."[20] If a large number of foreign supporters were interested in supporting a terrorist group, it is possible that sufficiently secure and anonymous cryptocurrencies would be a critical re-enabler of this funding stream by providing a channel for sending the money, and potentially by ensuring the anonymity and safety of the funders.

As is typical for an organization that is threatened, al Qaeda was forced to adapt or lose "market share" to other groups. Both of these events occurred: Following the crackdown on early al Qaeda funding streams and the military crackdown against its operations, the group began morphing into a more distributed movement, with funding streams that adapted to the different circumstances and opportunities available to the group. As Zarate explains, "Two years after 9/11 . . . our enemies [i.e., terrorist financiers] were beginning to adapt to the global pressure on the financial networks."[21] Similarly, "Al-Qaeda in the Islamic Maghrib (AQIM) . . . mastered the kidnapping-for-ransom business" and "the Al-Qaeda affiliate in Somalia, Al-Shabaab, created the most diversified and innovative funding method, a combination of taxes and checkpoint fees, diaspora remittances, and a charcoal trade-based money laundering scheme."[22]

These primarily territorial methods foreshadowed the evolution of al Qaeda in Iraq (AQI)—which "siphoned oil, extorted businesses, and robbed banks"—into ISIS, with its further focus on territorial funding.[23]

ISIS

ISIS has been primarily funded internally since its founding. In addition to utilizing methods pioneered and developed by its predecessor

---

[20] Zarate, 2013, p. 80.

[21] Zarate, 2013, p. 108.

[22] Zarate, 2013, pp. 362–363.

[23] Zarate, 2013, p. 362.

organization, ISIS took advantage of its territorial control to expand on these methods. ISIS's heavy reliance on territory, however, has left it vulnerable to more-traditional military and economic statecraft, blockades, being cut off from access to oil markets, and the like. Because of its significant isolation from international banking systems, ISIS has been even more reliant on cash—to the extent that U.S.-led attacks have been able to target physical storehouses of cash reserves.[24] Of course, this type of pressure can encourage the use of alternatives to cash.

The worsening financial condition of ISIS, along with its military losses, has many plausible outcomes, which is a recipe for further evolution. ISIS's transformation is ongoing, and the future needs and abilities of the group depend critically on the outcome. For example, despite ISIS's current violent opposition to many other terrorist groups, it might engage in occasional collaboration in illicit financial activities, leading to the further spread of innovative ways to evade CTF methods. We saw this feature of ISIS's transformation when it emerged from AQI, and it is perhaps more similar to the way Hezbollah diversified while its mainstay funding sources were under pressure, which we discuss further in the next section. This uncertainty makes monitoring and investigating the current and future financing activities of terrorist groups especially important.

Hezbollah

Hezbollah historically relied heavily on state funding from Iran, supplemented by income from international illegal activities and fundraising from sympathizers. State funding waned during the heavy sanctions regime against Iran, but during the suspension of sanctions (until the end of 2018), state funding was restored. Of course, newer sources of funding are unlikely to be abandoned.

The diverse sources that Hezbollah currently draws on include its own "dedicated entity specializing in worldwide drug trafficking and money laundering," as well as relationships with supporters and crimi-

24 Matthew Rosenberg, "U.S. Drops Bombs Not Just on ISIS, but on Its Cash, Too," *New York Times*, January 20, 2016.

nal organizations around the world that collaborate with or directly fund the organization.[25] Because of this diversity of funding sources, Hezbollah draws on the full gamut of criminal enterprises, from petty crime inside the United States, like "food stamp fraud, misuse of grocery store coupons, and sale of unlicensed T-shirts," to extortion in West Africa, to drug trafficking and fundraising in South America.[26]

Hezbollah's wide reach has made it a participant in the ongoing transfer of technology to other groups, primarily through training and supplying groups targeting Israel, but also through collaboration and trade with any convenient group, from the Hong Kong Mafia to otherwise archival Sunni groups.[27] These relationships of convenience make it likely that Hezbollah will be among the first terrorist organizations to use and spread new technologies.

Kickstarter-like funding has been pursued by groups in Gaza, perhaps serving as an example of technology and methods transfer.[28] Hezbollah subsequently ran a similar campaign.[29] Although these funding campaigns do not necessarily use cryptocurrency, the contact information is obtained via a signal address and the method of transferring funds would presumably need to be international and surreptitious, so cryptocurrency would be a good fit.

Narcoterrorist Organizations

Narcoterrorist organizations primarily rely on the narcotics trade for funds, although they are opportunistic about other sources of funds.

---

25 Levitt, 2016.

26 Matthew Levitt, *Hezbollah: The Global Footprint of Lebanon's Party of God*, Washington, D.C.: Georgetown University Press, 2013, pp. 334, 250, and 104–106, respectively.

27 Kim Cragin, Peter Chalk, Sara A. Daly, Brian A. Jackson, *Sharing the Dragon's Teeth: Terrorist Groups and the Exchange of New Technologies*, Santa Monica, Calif.: RAND Corporation, MG-485-DHS, 2007; Rex Hudson, *Terrorist and Organized Crime Groups in the Tri-Border Area (TBA) of South America*, Washington, D.C.: Library of Congress, Federal Research Division, 2003.

28 Lisa Daftari, "Hezbollah's New Crowdfunding Campaign: 'Equip a Mujahid,'" Foreign Desk, February 9, 2017; MEMRI Cyber and Jihad Lab, "Salafi-Jihadis Conduct Online 'Equip Us' Campaign to Raise Funds for Jihad in Gaza," December 16, 2015.

29 Daftari, 2017.

Although such groups are only marginally similar to the other groups we consider, their position in relation to those groups makes them a potential conduit for newer funding and money laundering methods.

Narcoterrorist groups have been under constant pressure from the international community for decades. Such pressure has resulted in an arms race of methods in smuggling, fighting, and finance and CTF. For these organizations, the potential for adaptation is less about sudden pressure than it is about new opportunities.

One troubling possibility is that there is potential for vertical consolidation in the illicit drug markets. This is an area where cryptocurrencies have already made significant inroads, although more in international retail markets than transnational smuggling, where narcoterrorists have historically been more active. In general, when organizations can eliminate intermediaries, their businesses become significantly more profitable. In this case, eliminating some of the middlemen might lead to a drastic reduction in risk for these groups because coordination is difficult and competition is brutal.

The primary potential digital avenue for narcotics traffickers to consolidate and cut out middlemen is by accessing darknet markets. These markets are already expanding as a mechanism for the distribution of drugs intranationally in many consumer countries and are used to facilitate international narcotics trade to a lesser extent.[30] This shift seems natural as an extension of current markets but could be a significant change for these organizations. It is unclear to what extent this may already be happening.

Lone-Wolf Attackers

Western citizens who are inspired by international terrorist groups are mostly self-financed and have not used fundraising in the past.[31] However, lone wolves and those traveling to join ISIS have raised funds via

---

30 Kristy Kruithof, Judith Aldridge, David Décary Hétu, Megan Sim, Elma Dujso, and Stijn Hoorens, *Internet-Facilitated Drugs Trade: An Analysis of the Size, Scope and the Role of the Netherlands*, Santa Monica, Calif.: RAND Corporation, RR-1607-WODC, 2016.

31 Daniel L. Byman, "How to Hunt a Lone Wolf: Countering Terrorists Who Act on Their Own," op-ed, Washington, D.C.: Brookings Institution, February 14, 2017.

appeals to their friends, raising the possibility that similar fundraising methods could use cryptocurrency and expand to funding attacks. It is plausible that financial support from outside organizations would be a force multiplier for the types of semi-directed attacks that ISIS has recently promoted.

Although cryptocurrency is not yet a viable way for this funding mode to be syndicated widely, this could change if technical barriers to use diminish. The diminishing technical barriers in cryptographically secure communication have led to new strategies for remote direction and supervision of these "independent" attacks.[32] Groups that currently attempt to direct attacks via secure conversations could instead pay for supplies remotely, or even order the supplies to be delivered to the would-be attacker, which would require much less initiative on the groups' part.

Conclusion

As of this writing, there is little indication that terrorist organizations are using cryptocurrency in any sort of extensive or systematic way. There are, however, lone-wolf actors and loosely associated groups that are likely to attempt, or are already attempting, to use these systems.[33] This is likely true regardless of the wisdom of doing so, as shown by the ill-informed (and ill-fated) claims of Ali Shukri Amin.[34] On the

[32] Rukmini Callimachi, "Not 'Lone Wolves' After All: How ISIS Guides World's Terror Plots from Afar," *New York Times*, February 4, 2017.

[33] Fergal Reid and Martin Harrigan, "An Analysis of Anonymity in the Bitcoin System," arXiv Physics and Society blog, Cornell University, May 7, 2012.

[34] In a grossly misinformed article, Ali Shukri Amin, writing under the pen-name Taqi'ul-Deen alMunthir, claimed that darkwaller allowed "totally anonymous" use of bitcoin, which would be accomplished if users "simply . . . set up a wallet and post their wallet address online" (Taqi'ulDeen alMunthir, "Bitcoin wa Sadaqat alJihad: Bitcoin and the Charity of Violent Physical Struggle," blog post, originally on Al Khila Faharidat Wordpress blog, 2014).

For an example of the consequences of such claims, see U.S. Department of Justice, "Virginia Teen Pleads Guilty to Providing Material Support to ISIL," Washington, D.C.: Office of Public Affairs, June 11, 2015.

other hand, despite claims to the contrary, there are "still only a small number of publicly-documented and confirmed cases of TF [terrorist finance] involving VCs [virtual currencies]."[35]

However, neither the technology nor the groups are static, and this might change the dynamics in the future. The incentives for finding alternatives discussed in this chapter are important, but the technical properties of cryptocurrency systems, as described in Chapter Three—which argue against the use of these systems by terrorist organizations—are likely to change in more-varied ways. This could make successful use of these technologies easier or harder. The question of whether terrorist organizations will use these systems is dependent on the available technology, as well as on these groups' needs and abilities. We will discuss these issues further in the remaining chapters.

---

35 Directorate General for Internal Policies, Policy Department for Citizens' Rights and Constitutional Affairs, *Virtual Currencies and Terrorist Financing: Assessing the Risks and Evaluating Responses*, Brussels: European Parliament, 2018, p. 9.

CHAPTER THREE

Limitations of Current Cryptocurrency Systems for Terrorist Use

In this chapter, we examine possible reasons for the current limited use of cryptocurrencies for organizational financing among terrorist groups. To do this, we examined six properties of these currencies that are limiting their use: anonymity, usability, security, acceptance, reliability, and volume. By *anonymity*, we mean the ability to hide and protect the identity of the user. *Usability* refers to the ease with which the user can conduct transactions and manage his or her own currency. *Security* refers to the degree to which the cryptocurrency infrastructure secures the confidentiality, integrity, and accuracy of transactions and user accounts. By *acceptance*, we mean the degree to which the currency is accepted by a user community as well as the size of the community of users. *Reliability* refers to the speed and availability of transactions, as viewed by users. Finally, *volume* refers to the time-averaged aggregate size of transactions in the cryptocurrency infrastructure.

We describe these properties in the context of cryptocurrencies and discuss each with respect to terrorist use. Although we discuss each property individually, we recognize that the properties are closely linked. For example, anonymity would be boosted if the currencies were easier to use securely, or if the volume were much greater, making terrorist use less conspicuous. Similarly, volume would increase if the currency were accepted in more places and were more reliable for consumers.

For a brief primer on the cryptocurrencies discussed in this chapter, please see the appendix to this report.

Anonymity

How anonymous a cryptocurrency is depends on many factors, both operational and technical. To understand this concept, we focus first on Bitcoin and then discuss differences in other systems. Recall that both Bitcoin and other cryptocurrencies are, in a technical sense, not "owned" by people or institutions. Instead, cryptocurrencies are controlled by whoever has the (assumedly secret) cryptographic private keys to which the funds were sent. For example, if the owner of a key gives the private key to another person, the new person could spend the money, but so could the first person if they kept a copy of the keys. The owner of a key can be identified only by the corresponding public key. For this reason, Bitcoin is frequently called pseudonymous because identities are masked by the keys, but this is somewhat misleading. The owner of a key could be well known if they publish their public key to allow others to send them money, and even if not, they could be identified using a variety of methods, which we describe further below.

For example, if someone were to use a single public/private key pair for all of their transactions (known as "key reuse"), it would be relatively easy for an observer to discover their identity: The person who spent 10,000 bitcoins from the public key "1XPTgDRhN8RFnzni-WCddobD9iKZatrvH4" on a now-famous pair of pizzas on May 22, 2010,[1] demonstrating the first real-world purchase using bitcoin, is the same person who sent 1,300 bitcoins to "1DvSvCnRsHdrA76PnD-1j58wAeUFnhTauxJ" on November 15, 2010.[2] The fact that the first transaction is tied to the person's real-world identity means that the second transaction is as well. This would be an operational failure for anonymity; key reuse is discouraged by the Bitcoin community, and public discussion of the accounts involved makes tracing the transaction on the public blockchain trivial.

Even without any key reuse between transactions, it is possible to find users who control multiple accounts because the outputs are used

---

1   Eric Mack, "The Bitcoin Pizza Purchase That's Worth $7 Million Today," *Forbes*, December 23, 2013.

2   Benjamin Wallace, "The Rise and Fall of Bitcoin," *Wired*, November 23, 2011.

together for a single purchase. Reid and Harrigan, who first performed this type of analysis, note many other threats to Bitcoin user anonymity that can potentially identify users, including temporal data, off-network information, internet protocol (IP) address data, and other side channels.[3] There has been much work on "deanonymization" using a variety of methods, and even transactions that are not yet able to be deanonymized are plausibly susceptible, given future (or nonpublic) capabilities.

Users can mitigate some of these technical threats to anonymity, as well as threats to the security of the currencies, by using techniques that are built into some newer Bitcoin applications or by taking steps to use Bitcoin more anonymously, such as using coin "mixing" to hide ownership or obfuscating IP addresses. Recent research focuses on countering various Bitcoin tumbling schemes that remix coins and make identification more difficult, including the TumbleBit scheme, which is compatible with Bitcoin today.[4] Many such methods can be used by the technically proficient, if they are willing to find tools for doing so and are comfortable verifying that the tools are secure. However, defending against all threats requires significant technical knowledge and following best practices very consistently; new methods for deanonymizing users, such as CoinJoin Sudoku, continue to be developed.[5]

Additionally, many potential operational methods of evading detection, like using TOR to hide IP addresses when using Bitcoin, have subtle flaws.[6] It is therefore difficult for users to know when they

---

[3] Reid and Harrigan, 2012.

[4] Ethan Heilman, Leen AlShenibr, Foteini Baldimtsi, Alessandra Scafuro, and Sharon Goldberg, "TumbleBit: An Untrusted Bitcoin-Compatible Anonymous Payment Hub," International Association for Cryptologic Research, 2016. TumbleBit is a protocol that mixes transactions among various parties to hide identities.

[5] This attack uses the fact that inputs and outputs from each participant in mixing must match to identify individuals that participated, based on matching the inputs and outputs. See Kristov Atlas, "Weak Privacy Guarantees for SharedCoin Mixing Service," security advisory blog post, June 9, 2014a.

[6] TOR is an internet infrastructure that obscures users' network activity and location, which improves anonymity. Alex Biryukov and Ivan Pustogarov, "Bitcoin over Tor Isn't a

have been successful at evading deanonymization and detection. For this reason, Bitcoin is not trustworthy as anonymous in the face of technically sophisticated adversaries. Even with a cryptocurrency that is more effectively anonymous than Bitcoin, there are no guarantees that anonymity will stand up to concerted efforts to attack it.

Non-Bitcoin cryptocurrencies incorporate a variety of mechanisms to boost their anonymity by obfuscating transactions. DarkCoin (now Dash) employs the type of mixing discussed earlier by default, as do several other coins. These coins employ a variety of other methods for masking ownership, such as standard denominations to hide transaction amounts. Despite this, other avenues of deanonymization exist.[7] The cryptonote protocol uses a cryptographic technique called "ring signatures" that enables pseudonym reuse while making it more difficult to associate it with a user spending money.[8] This approach masks which public key was used for a transaction, making the blockchain a less public ledger. Modifications of this concept have been implemented that also allow transaction amounts to be obfuscated.[9] Monero, the largest of these currencies, bills itself as "Secure, Private, and Untraceable" and has begun to gain adoption in online darknet markets for drugs, although it has only a small percentage of the value of Bitcoin.[10] IP masking, which has been incorporated into Monero, is another technique to boost anonymity. Monero is, however, only the latest in a series of purportedly anonymous cryptocurrencies that seem poised to gain significant market share; others are Dash, BlackCoin, ShadowCash, and Zcash. Each has adherents, but none has found the

7 Kristov Atlas, *An Analysis of Darkcoin's Blockchain Privacy via Darksend+*, September 19, 2014b.

8 Joseph K. Liu, Victor K. Wei, and Duncan S. Wong, "Linkable Spontaneous Anonymous Group Signature for Ad Hoc Groups," Sydney, Australia: Information Security and Privacy 9th Australasian Conference, July 13–15, 2004, pp. 325–335.

9 Shen Noether, "Ring Signature Confidential Transactions for Monero," Cryptology ePrint Archive, November 11, 2015.

10 Yuji Nakamura, "New Digital Currency Spikes as Drug Dealers Get More Secrecy," Bloomberg News, August 29, 2016.

Good Idea," paper presented at the 2015 Institute of Electrical and Electronics Engineers Symposium on Security and Privacy, San Jose, Calif., May 18–20, 2015a.

widespread adoption that Bitcoin, Ethereum, and other legal and less anonymous currencies have. Widespread adoption, in turn, comes with more acceptance and greater volume and also drives greater developer focus on usability. Usability, in turn, enables more terrorists to contemplate using cryptocurrencies, rather than a few technically adept members of the organizations.

Usability

Like many emerging technologies, cryptocurrencies are difficult for newcomers to use.[11] Such easy-to-use alternatives as online wallets that manage funds for the user are problematic for surreptitious use because the service can both see details of what is being done and freeze funds; such wallets are similar to banks in that they are subject to anti–money laundering regulations. The regulatory approach in different jurisdictions and typical use patterns will be critical to understanding this in the future.

Methods of managing cryptocurrency anonymously require somewhat more technical sophistication, but general trends indicate that the technical sophistication of both users and the public is increasing, while cryptocurrency developers are increasing usability and working on making these systems more secure.[12] For example, Kristov Atlas published a book on using Bitcoin anonymously that is relatively user-friendly for those who are technically adept.[13] On the other hand, use of techniques that allow anonymity might, paradoxically, function as a "red flag" for intelligence services monitoring the use of these currencies. Additionally, even the use of sophisticated techniques will not necessarily provide anonymity in the face of a sophisticated opponent.

---

[11] Nate Lanxon and Adam Satariano, "Hardly Anyone Paying the Hackers? Because Using Bitcoin Is Hard," Bloomberg News, May 15, 2017.

[12] Katharina Krombholz, Aljosha Judmayer, Matthias Gusenbauer, and Edgar Weippl, "The Other Side of the Coin: User Experiences with Bitcoin Security and Privacy," Financial Cryptography and Data Security 2016 Conference, Barbados, February 22–26, 2016.

[13] Kristov Atlas, *Anonymous Bitcoin: How to Keep Your [Bitcoin] All to Yourself,* self-published, 2015.

Security

Closely related to usability is security; as noted previously, there are trade-offs between them. Security is a critical need for any user of a monetary system, and cryptocurrencies have many potential weaknesses that traditional currencies do not share. For example, many formerly centrally run cryptocurrency exchanges, which allowed users to easily create online wallets, have been compromised. These compromises—both insider-driven and external—led to well-publicized losses of user funds. This type of loss is far from unknown in traditional banking, but the procedures for handling it make these losses unlikely to affect depositors.

The alternative to such centrally run systems is user-controlled wallets. The use of such wallets requires the user to secure the system. Hardware wallets, which allow users to store currencies in a dedicated device, are susceptible to a variety of attacks, from the highly technical to simple theft, and software wallets require the user to secure the system being used to store them.[14] A compromise of the computer system could easily lead to a complete loss of funds; even in 2011, early in Bitcoin's history, some computer viruses were found that stole bitcoin.[15] Most users are not capable of fully securing a computer or smartphone holding cryptocurrency, and in other domains, even well-protected, fully offline systems have been hacked by sophisticated adversaries.

In addition to hacking, there is a possibility of protocol-level vulnerabilities: If there is a flaw in the software, or in the logic of how the system works, it could be exploited. Even if the code is secure, the standard assumption in cryptography is that systems and algorithms become less secure over time as flaws and attacks against the system

---

14 Miron Cuperman (devrandom) and Chris Taylor, "The Problem with Bitcoin Hardware Wallets (and possible solutions)," GitHub draft, March 9, 2014.

15 Adrian Covert, "There's a Virus That Will Steal All Your Bitcoins," Gizmodo.com, June 17, 2011.

are found; it is likely that this also would apply to cryptocurrency.[16] As alternative cryptocurrencies become more widespread, attract academic interest, and become valuable enough for attackers to want to steal, they are likely to experience the same types of attacks that have been waged against Bitcoin. For example, the ring signature schemes used in some cryptocurrencies have been found to provide no anonymity, leaving the systems vulnerable to attack.[17]

It is unclear how difficult it will be to use these currencies securely in the future. We expect that concerns about security will decrease over time if no such breaches occur. Nonetheless, terrorist groups still might not trust these systems, especially because they are largely designed and maintained by people working in Western countries.

Acceptance

The limited reach of cryptocurrencies at present is a significant challenge, especially in the regions where terrorist groups operate. For example, despite the large network of Bitcoin-accepting vendors and services, there are few Bitcoin ATMs in the Middle East; outside of Israel, the only such ATM operating as of January 2018 was a deposit-only ATM in Jubail, Saudi Arabia, with a deposit limit of $500–$600.[18] The future trajectory of these currency technologies is uncertain, but if and when consumer use increases across the world, it will make use by terrorists much more plausible. Generally, however, the conditions needed to allow terrorist groups to establish themselves and flourish,

---

16 Because current transactions are secured with a given level of security, with a specific key size and algorithm, increasing computational power and attacks against the methods used will reduce that security. Typically, systems are upgraded to use more-recent and more-secure algorithms and larger and more-secure key lengths, but this cannot guard the anonymity of past transactions.

17 Shen Noether, "Broken Crypto in Shadowcash," archived shnoe Wordpress blog, February 11, 2016.

18 Suhail Abboushi, "Global Virtual Currency—Brief Overview," *Journal of Applied Business and Economics*, Vol. 19, No. 6, 2017; "Bitcoin ATM Location Profile," coinlocations. com, undated.

such as failed states and lack of government oversight, might make the technological infrastructure needed for cryptocurrencies infeasible.[19]

Reliability

The newness and instability of cryptocurrency as a whole, and of specific cryptocurrencies, might create concerns about reliability. Bitcoin's price instability is the obvious example, but additional reliability issues exist—especially if support for the currency declines—and could lead to developers abandoning a project or a lack of commercial support by exchanges. Most cryptocurrencies that have been launched are abandoned or shut down, some because of neglect, and others because of scams or attacks.

These problems are less severe for short-term uses, which cover many potential uses by terrorist groups. The stability of a cryptocurrency system depends on typical market risks and the continuing involvement of developers, interest of miners, and the ecosystem of applications that support the currency.[20] For this reason, it is unclear how many of the newer cryptocurrencies will last.[21] These factors matter primarily in the medium-to-long term, not in the short term, when money would be transferred in and out of such a currency quickly.

---

19 Dominic Lisanti, "Do Failed States Really Breed Terrorists? An Examination of Terrorism in Sub-Saharan Africa Comparing Statistical Approaches with a Fuzzy Set Qualitative Comparative Analysis," CAPERS Workshop, New York, New York University, May 14, 2010; Robert I. Rotberg, "Failed States in a World of Terror," *Foreign Affairs*, July 1, 2002.

20 *Mining* is the process by which transactions are irreversibly locked into the blockchain so that transactions cannot be altered later. Those who participate in the mining process (i.e., miners) compete to find the solution to a very difficult cryptographic function, called a "hash function."

21 As of the beginning of 2017, five of the ten largest cryptocurrencies by market cap are less than two years old.

Volume

Transaction volume is a critical limitation for reliable transfer. Low volume makes the price more sensitive to transactions and makes the transfer of large amounts of money expensive; the price increases when the currency is purchased by those trying to transfer the money and drops again when it is sold at the other end. Because of this, large transaction volumes are important for any terrorist group attempting to use a particular cryptocurrency. This is a particularly critical concern for smaller and newer cryptocurrencies, in addition to concerns about the security and reliability of any new system.

The other critical problem with low volume is the traceability of transactions. This problem manifests in two ways. As mentioned earlier, large transactions have impacts on price; demand increases are reflected in publicly visible prices, making the transaction nonanonymous. In addition, a public ledger, even one with robust technical anonymity, cannot mask the fact that large volumes or high-value single transactions appear. Because transactions are posted publicly for all to see (including law enforcement), changes in average volume are easy to detect. Thus, a sudden spike in volume is enough to attract attention.

Implications of the Properties of Cryptocurrencies

These technical aspects of cryptocurrencies are important to terrorist organizations, but which aspects matter most depend on how groups attempt to use them. In Table 3.1, we provide an estimate of the relative importance of these properties for the activities discussed in Chapter Two. Each box is scored and shaded as of "critical importance" (gray), "moderate importance" (light gray), or "lesser importance" (white). By *critical importance*, we mean that the cryptocurrency property is essential to the terrorist activity, and without the property, the activity could not be supported. By *moderate importance*, we mean that the cryptocurrency property is moderately important to the terrorist activity, because either the property has an impact on only a subset of the activities, or there are work-arounds that allow the terrorist activities to be supported. Finally, by *lesser importance*, we mean that the cryptocurrency property may be convenient, but its absence has little impact on the terrorist activity.

Fundraising

For fundraising, the anonymity of donors and recipients is moderately important. In some nations, it is illegal to provide material support to known terrorist organizations, which could serve as a deterrent to donors. Recipients likewise may require anonymity, particularly from the authorities. Usability—or the ease of individual use and management of funds—is critically important to donors and recipients alike. Security is moderately important for fundraising, which would ensure that funds are not lost to interception. Acceptance and reliability are relatively convenient but are less important with regard to fundraising, because only the donor and recipient require access to the cryptocurrency infrastructure, incomplete transactions could be re-initiated, and price instability would have an impact only when the recipient sought to spend the donations for the organization's needs. Finally, volume is moderately important for this activity, particularly because the ability of a cryptocurrency to support (and hide) large-scale transactions would enable deep-pocketed donors to make large donations to a terrorist organization.

Illegal Drug and Arms Trafficking

For illegal drug and arms trafficking, terrorist organizations require anonymity and high security to avoid detection by the authorities during and after the transaction. Usability is relatively convenient but less important, because a small set of individuals with the skills to use the currencies would be required on either end of the transaction. Likewise, widespread acceptance of the cryptocurrency is convenient but less important because only a few people engage in these transactions. The reliability of the cryptocurrency is moderately important, mostly because transaction partners may have little trust in one another, and problems with transactions could be erroneously attributed to intentional deceit, fatally disrupting the transaction. Finally, although some illegal drug and arms transactions might be large, we rate volume as less important in the cryptocurrency infrastructure because users may be presumed sophisticated enough to hide large transactions in a series of smaller transactions.

Remittance and Transfer

For remittance and transfer activities, as with fundraising, anonymity is moderately important in order to avoid attention and detection by the authorities. Usability is convenient but less important because few users are required to remit or transfer funds and can presumably acquire the skills needed to do so. Security, on the other hand, is very important for this activity, because the remitted or transferred funds will likely be in large amounts and be vulnerable to theft or detection. Wide acceptance is convenient but less important because the number of users engaging in these transactions will likely be small. However, both reliability and volume are very important for this activity because assured transfer of large amounts (with stable currency) is routinely required.

Attack Funding

For attack funding, anonymity—particularly, the anonymity of the attacker—is highly important to avoid detection prior to the operation. Usability is convenient but less important; we assess that attackers and their handlers would be motivated to acquire the skills needed to employ cryptocurrencies to remit funds. Like anonymity, security is highly important to avoid revealing the planned attack prior to its execution. We assess wide acceptance to be moderately important because access to the cryptocurrency infrastructure may otherwise be delimiting. Reliability is very important, because transfer of funds to support attacks may be time-sensitive and may be disrupted if prices are unstable (particularly exchange rates with fiat currencies). Finally, volume is convenient but less important because most terrorist attack operations are relatively low-cost and involve few people.

Operational Funding

Operational funding—that is, funding the day-to-day operations of the terrorist organization—will require relatively less anonymity, because most transactions will involve mundane (and mostly legal) support. Likewise, usability is convenient but less important; transactions will likely occur in relatively controlled conditions and among a limited set of users who can presumably obtain the necessary skills. Security of both the transactions and management of the funds is highly important because amounts would be relatively large and the structure of the organizational funding would reveal the scope and scale of the operation. Acceptance is moderately important because operational funding would involve transactions with periphery organizations providing services (such as food, communications, etc.). Likewise, the reliability of the cryptocurrency and its infrastructure would be moderately important to support trust among transaction partners and ensure budgetary coherence in the face of unstable prices. Finally, volume is highly important because supporting operations is likely the largest ongoing expense to the organization and thus would require large dollar amounts.

Table 3.1
Assessment of Terrorist Finance Activities with Respect to Cryptocurrency Properties

	Fundraising	Illegal Drug and Arms Trafficking	Remittance and Transfer	Attack Funding	Operational Funding
Anonymity	Moderate importance	Critical importance	Moderate importance	Critical importance	Lesser importance
Usability	Critical importance	Lesser importance	Lesser importance	Lesser importance	Lesser importance
Security	Moderate importance	Critical importance	Critical importance	Critical importance	Critical importance
Acceptance	Lesser importance	Lesser importance	Lesser importance	Moderate importance	Moderate importance
Reliability	Lesser importance	Moderate importance	Lesser importance	Critical importance	Moderate importance
Volume	Moderate importance	Lesser importance	Critical importance	Lesser importance	Critical importance

Conclusion

Security in the cryptocurrency infrastructure is of moderate to high importance for terrorist organizations, yet current cryptocurrencies are vulnerable to a variety of cyberattacks, as we discuss in the next chapter. Even newer currencies that are thought to improve security are subject to significant scrutiny as new security vulnerabilities are discovered over time. When we consider all our assessments together, including such other important properties as the reliability and volume of the cryptocurrency market, we find that no current cryptocurrency can address all of the terrorist organizations' financial needs. However, we note that, particularly with improved usability, cryptocurrencies such as Bitcoin may be appealing to use in fundraising, and some evidence is emerging that terrorist organizations may be using cryptocurrencies for this purpose.[22] Thus, we conclude that current cryptocurrencies are generally not well matched with the totality of features that would be needed and desirable to the terrorist groups examined.

However, that does not preclude the use of cryptocurrencies for such activities as fundraising, for which Bitcoin might provide an attractive path as usability enhancements are made. Nonetheless, all terrorist organization finance activities require moderate or high security, and no current cryptocurrency could likely provide the requisite required security. Given the importance of security, we discuss the vulnerabilities of cryptocurrencies in the next chapter.

---

[22] Steven Stalinsky, "The Cryptocurrency-Terrorism Connection Is Too Big to Ignore," *Washington Post*, December 17, 2018.

CHAPTER FOUR

Cyberattacks on Cryptocurrency

Given the importance of security to terrorist organizational finance, as described in the previous chapter, it is worth discussing several of the technical attacks that law enforcement and others could use to thwart the surreptitious use of cryptocurrency by terrorist organizations. Most of the challenge to terrorist use of cryptocurrencies comes from sophisticated countries, which "have a level of expertise and sophistication sufficient to discover new vulnerabilities in systems and to exploit them."[1] The attacks discussed in this chapter almost all require that level of sophistication.[2]

The problems terrorist organizations might face from their adversaries, therefore, are potentially considerable. Importantly, only a few of these attacks are available to significantly less sophisticated actors, as we note.

---

[1] James R. Gosler and Lewis Von Thaer, *Task Force Report: Resilient Military Systems and the Advanced Cyber Threat*, Washington, D.C.: Defense Science Board, U.S. Department of Defense, January 2013, p. 41.

[2] The attacks discussed require much less capability than at least some Western governments are capable of deploying. As Gosler and Von Thaer note, "Tiers V and VI attackers can invest large amounts of money (billions) and time (years) to *actually create* vulnerabilities in systems, including systems that are otherwise strongly protected." But attackers "will usually try lower-tier exploits first before exposing their most advanced capabilities," so the lower tier is the most salient (2013, p. 2).

Classification of Attacks Against Cryptocurrency Use

Several different types of attacks could be mounted against a crypto-currency system. The types of attack that are most important in this context are (1) deanonymization, (2) spending denial, (3) theft, and (4) systemic attacks. *Deanonymization*, which we discussed in the previous chapter, involves revealing the identity of cryptocurrency users. *Spending denial* involves preventing certain transactions from being processed by the network or included in the blockchain. Once a target is known, this type of attack could allow an adversary to make the terrorist organization's money unspendable, either temporarily or permanently. *Theft*, on the other hand, requires the compromise or theft of the private key of the targeted individual or the compromise of other aspects of the cryptography underlying the system.[3] The most drastic type of attack is a *systemic attack*, one that shuts down the network running the blockchain, thereby stopping the use of the system for all users.

We also classify attack types in terms of their visibility as offline, passive, active, and blatant.

Offline attacks are ways to deanonymize transactions without participating in the system at all, which includes most types of statistical and side-channel attacks. These can occur in real time but require no connection to the blockchain.

Passive attacks require data collection but not activity that interferes with the system or action that is noticeable to typical outside observers. For instance, to collect the IP addresses of individuals transmitting transactions, an adversary might run a Bitcoin node or nodes, or collect internet traffic data. Similarly, by participating in coin-mix systems, an attacker could reduce the resulting anonymity advantage.

Active attacks require specific, but surreptitious, involvement in the system. This may include some "spending denial" attacks, in which

---

3   For a discussion of compromised algorithms underlying the cryptographic protocols (primitives) as they relate to Bitcoin, see Ilias Giechaskiel, Cas Cremers, and Kasper B. Rasmussen, "On Bitcoin Security in the Presence of Broken Cryptographic Primitives," Heraklion, Greece: 21st European Symposium on Research in Computer Security, September 26–30, 2016, pp. 201–222.

someone is prevented from having a transaction approved. These attacks, while potentially or obviously detectable by the attacked party, are not obvious to an outside observer. A simple version of such an attack involves guessing or stealing a password, but these attacks also can be very complex.

Blatant attacks, as the name implies, are clearly visible to the public or the target. These attacks include distributed denial of service (DDoS) attacks against a user's computer, taking down servers, or compromising a currency exchange or an online wallet provider to seize or redirect the funds of a target. This is the primary means to carry out a systemic attack: The action, and typically the result, is public. The Flame attack, a sophisticated blatant attack, exploited a problem with Microsoft's verification of software updates, a fact that was not possible to hide once the attack was found.[4]

Table 4.1 summarizes the main types of attacks against cryptocurrencies and their characteristics.

Sophisticated Attacks

Very sophisticated attack vectors also exist. These vectors can provide a broad set of capabilities and attack methods for the most sophisticated actors and could make any of the attack types easier. Sophisticated attacks include *software supply chain attacks*, *backdoors*, and *cryptographic attacks*.

In a *software supply chain attack*, a vulnerability is introduced into the system by an attacker somewhere in the supply chain prior to the ultimate target. An example of this is the 2017 NotPetya attacks, which were disguised as ransomware but actually were simpler attacks against targeted computer systems located mostly in Ukraine. One vector for the infection was a supply chain attack, in which a software update server was hacked, and then the attackers distributed the virus to the targets disguised as a legitimate update.[5]

---

4 Kim Zetter, "Flame Hijacks Microsoft Update to Spread Malware Disguised as Legit Code," *Wired*, June 4, 2012.

5 Eliad Kimhy, "NotPetya Intrusion Vectors and Propagation," Cybereason Intelligence Team, June 30, 2017.

Table 4.1
Types of Attacks Against Cryptocurrencies and Their Characteristics

	Offline	Passive	Active	Blatant
Deanonymization	Yes—i.e., Coinjoin Sudoku	Snooping IP addresses, other monitoring	User attack[a] and mixer participation deanonymization	Various
Spending denial	User attack[a]	No	User attack[a] and compromise 50% or more of hashpower	Public fork threats and DDoS[a]
Theft	No	No	Compromised cryptoprimitives and user attack[a] (surreptitious theft of private keys)	Attacks on hosted wallets[a] and compromised cryptoprimitives
Systemic attack	No	No	"Accidental" downtime[a] and software supply chain attacks	DDoS[a] and targeted border gateway protocol attacks[a]

[a] Potentially available to less sophisticated attackers.

A *backdoor* is a software vulnerability introduced purposefully to allow an attacker access at a later time. For example, Juniper Networks, a firewall and networking equipment vendor, experienced a backdoor and a cryptographic vulnerability in some of their products introduced through a supply chain attack. The backdoor allowed the attacker to access and control the devices once they were purchased from Juniper and installed, and also to decrypt supposedly encrypted traffic.[6]

A *cryptographic attack* allows an attacker to significantly reduce or eliminate the security provided by encryption. This approach is especially powerful in the case of cryptocurrency and could allow theft, counterfeiting, or almost any other type of attack against the system. In the case of the previously mentioned Juniper Networks attack, a vulnerability allowed decryption of encrypted traffic by changing the source code, thus introducing a hard-to-detect cryptographic vulner-

6   Bruce Schneier, "Details About Juniper's Firewall Backdoor," Schneier on Security blog, April 19, 2016.

ability into the encryption scheme.[7] There are methods to circumvent the possibility of many of these attacks, such as by transmitting private keys to transactions as a means of transferring money outside of the blockchain to avoid computer-based theft of the keys, but such methods are, at best, difficult to implement.

Usefulness of Different Attack Types Against Terrorist Organizations

In addition to considering the classes of attack, their sophistication, and their visibility, we wanted to understand how useful different attack types are as a way to attack terrorist organizations. This can be understood by considering the vulnerabilities, threats, and impact associated with each class of attack. In this discussion, it is helpful to differentiate between the direct effects of an attack on terrorist organizations, the future implications of the attack, and the uncertainty created because of not knowing what types of attacks are available to the organizations' adversaries.

Spending Denial

A simple spending denial attack would be obvious to the account holder; attackers would continually block transactions, thus ensuring that no currency is spent. The attacker could create an economic incentive for cryptocurrency miners to disallow certain transactions or not include a transaction in the blockchain; the miners, in turn, would commit to forking (splitting) the blockchain if a particular account spends money in a transaction. This type of attack requires significant computational power and would be public. Similarly, temporary spending denial is possible by attacking the Bitcoin network as a whole, attacking the nodes connecting the key owner to the internet, or completely disabling their internet access.

A much simpler and more surreptitious alternative would be to delete or otherwise corrupt the keys that allow access to the account;

---

7 Schneier, 2016.

if those keys are rendered inaccessible (and backups do not exist), the money would be unusable. This type of attack could be offline, or at least not visibly online, although the target would know that he or she lost access. On the other hand, such an attack would require significantly more information about the users' systems, operational setup, and/or location. Additionally, proper key backup and operational security could frustrate this class of attack.

Theft

A different tactic that can be used against a cryptocurrency user, whether licit or illicit, is to hack their computer or get access to their cryptographic keys and submit transactions to transfer the currency into a different account. This form of theft has been demonstrated repeatedly in various forms.[8] Such an attack can take the form of compromising the cryptographic keys to the account, either via exfiltration (stealing) or by exploiting cryptographic weaknesses. Alternatively, such an attack could involve compromising the security of the computer being used for the transactions. These attacks would need to be active but might not be particularly obvious or provable; funds can be stolen so that the attack is not obvious to anyone but the target.

Systemic Attacks

There is a variety of attacks that can temporarily or permanently make a blockchain inaccessible or inoperable. This could be accomplished by an attack on the systems the blockchain relies on, such as internet architecture, but such an attack could cause significant collateral damage because it would affect a large swath of the internet.[9] Alternatively, a DDoS attack, if large enough, could prevent the use of the system as a whole indefinitely, either by disabling key parts of internet infrastructure or by attacking bitcoin miners directly. Such an attack

8   Luke Parker, "Bitcoin Stealing Malware Evolves Again," Bravenewcoin.com, February 11, 2016.

9   Maria Apostolaki, Aviv Zohar, and Laurent Vanbever, "Hijacking Bitcoin: Large-Scale Network Attacks on Cryptocurrencies," Arxiv.org, May 2016.

would require much less sophistication and would be harder to attribute, if deniability is desired.

Backdoors and Software Supply Chain

Much attention has been given to the threat of "50-percent attacks" on a blockchain network, which would allow a variety of both obvious and nonobvious attacks.[10] These types of attacks have been considered to be infeasible against large networks, such as Bitcoin, but this is not necessarily true. For example, attackers could compromise mining pools instead of building hash power themselves—as they did in 2014.[11] This could be done surreptitiously via software supply chain or mining server attacks, especially if the compromised servers were used for nonobvious attacks, such as spending denial or deanonymization. At one point in 2014, a single pool controlled more than 50 percent of the network hash power; while the network has become more decentralized, it has long been the case that fewer than six pools control significantly more than half of the total hash power.[12]

Confidence Attacks

The perceived sophistication of actors and the unclear level of security in any cryptocurrency system ensure that confidence plays a critical role. Because of the history of weaknesses in cryptographic systems, whether technical or nontechnical, there is a concern that backdoors might have been introduced (intentionally or accidentally) in the cryptographic primitives used to secure these systems, in the system's hardware or software, or in the random number generators used by the

---

[10] Fifty-percent attacks mean that more than 50 percent of the miners control the blockchain hash rate (i.e., computing power), allowing these controlling miners to introduce incorrect information into the blockchain in order to steal bitcoins or perpetrate other malfeasance.

[11] Andy Greenberg, "Hacker Redirects Traffic from 19 Internet Providers to Steal Bitcoin," *Wired*, August 7, 2014.

[12] Joel Hruska, "One Bitcoin Group Now Controls 51% of Total Mining Power, Threatening Entire Currency's Safety," Extremetech.com, June 16, 2014.

system.[13] This concern exists despite a history of significant surreptitious criminal use of cryptographic systems; it would be difficult for terrorist organizations to be confident that the backdoors or discovered vulnerabilities that could compromise their funds are not being held in reserve for exactly such a use.

Differences in Vulnerabilities for More Sophisticated Cryptocurrencies

As mentioned earlier, there are still significant downsides to these more sophisticated cryptographic techniques, starting with the fact that they are not well tested. Therefore, new vulnerabilities may emerge as threats both to anonymity and to the security of the currency itself. Cryptographic security varies over time as new attacks are uncovered and as previously strong cryptosystems become susceptible to newer cryptanalytic techniques and faster computers.

Despite this concern, it is unlikely that efforts to secure cryptocurrencies will disappear even if such newer cryptocurrencies as Zcash or Monero fail; anonymous transactions equivalent to Zcash offline transfers also have been used on the Ethereum blockchain, and ring signatures are in use in other systems.[14]

There is a case to be made that Zcash and related systems will enable more convenient and easier enforcement of anti–money laundering laws than current cryptocurrencies—or even than current national currencies. If it is implemented in conjunction with authorities, the infrastructure that enables view keys and transactions that can be private while retaining provable ownership could be a boon to law enforcement. On the other hand, it is very possible for an implementation of the same technology to be designed to avoid law enforcement and enable easier money laundering.

13 Thomas C. Hales, "The NSA Back Door to NIST," *Notices of the AMS*, Vol. 61, No. 2, February 2014, pp. 190–192. *A cryptographic primitive* is a low-level algorithm used to build a cryptographic protocol.

14 Sean Bowe, "zkSNARKs in Ethereum," Zcash blog, July 28, 2016.

Conclusion

In the near future, the available classes of attacks seem to show that there are few ways in which terrorist organizations can confidently use cryptocurrency systems anonymously because deanonymization is always plausible. At the same time, there are few ways for terrorist organizations to be stopped without clearly alerting them that they have been discovered. These advantages and disadvantages mean that there is real potential for terrorist groups to use cryptocurrencies for *some* purposes, despite little to no evidence that they are currently doing so and even though there is reason to think that terrorist groups would be hesitant to rely on these systems. Because of this uncertainty, it is important to continue monitoring these systems for signs that significant terrorist use is becoming more plausible. We discuss this issue in the next chapter.

CHAPTER FIVE

Future Viability of Cryptocurrencies

As terrorist methods and cryptocurrencies develop, the utility of these approaches and systems for terrorist organizations remains unclear. Nevertheless, there are many factors that could signal an uptick in the importance of cryptocurrencies to terrorist organizations. We expect that there will be some use of cryptocurrencies by terrorist groups, but the extent of that use will depend on the viability of these systems.

The primary factors that will increase viability for use by terrorist organizations are broader use, better anonymity, lax or inconsistent regulation with associated improved security, and adoption in adjacent markets. Conversely, the primary factors that will decrease viability for use by terrorist organizations are continued instability and infighting in the community, robust international regulation and law enforcement in conjunction with the intelligence community, and increasing or continuing security breaches and hacks of systems. We briefly discuss each of these factors in this chapter.

Factors Increasing the Viability of Cryptocurrency Use

Broader Use of Cryptocurrency

A first indicator that cryptocurrency is becoming more feasible for use by terrorist organizations is that the market continues to grow. A growing market presumably will require increased reliability of the system and more-widespread usage. Growth will increase the volume of transactions—a critical limitation of current systems—and greater adoption of these systems will spur improvements in ease of use. As use becomes more common across the world, the current lack of acceptance of these systems, especially in areas where terrorist organizations operate, could disappear.

More Use of Anonymous Cryptocurrencies

Widespread adoption of second-generation cryptocurrencies with advanced privacy features will enable more illicit use of these systems. The competition among cryptocurrencies has led to a huge first-mover advantage for Bitcoin. Its status as the original cryptocurrency, combined with the current size of the market, makes it difficult for altcoins to gain significant traction.

Currently, despite an increase in their use, altcoins are not a large part of the total cryptocurrency market, which is still almost completely dominated by Bitcoin. Monero, which was launched as a more privacy conscious alternative to Bitcoin, has seen its value increase significantly, although it is still worth less than 2 percent of Bitcoin's value.[1] The even more recent Zcash is worth only 10 percent of that amount, which is clearly insufficient for it to be more than a minor part of the total cryptocurrency ecosystem, both for criminals and for legitimate users.

Because CTF is used heavily to "make it harder for individuals . . . financing terrorist organizations to access the formal financial system," pseudonymity and unlinkable transactions are particularly worrisome characteristics of the cryptocurrency system.[2] Zarate notes that "this strategy [to deter future donors] required ensuring that such financiers understood there could be a dangerous, direct cost to them and their financial futures if they continued to finance these activities."[3]

1   Andy Greenberg, "Monero, the Drug Dealer's Cryptocurrency of Choice, Is on Fire," *Wired*, January 25, 2017.

2   Zarate, 2013, p. 41.

3   Zarate, 2013, p. 109.

Lax or Inconsistent Regulatory Oversight

Another indicator of increased viability is lax or inconsistent regulatory oversight. At the time of this writing, regulatory oversight in the United States, Europe, and China makes it difficult to obtain bitcoin anonymously on an exchange. The regulatory oversight, however, is somewhat limited: In the United States, oversight does not cover non-exchange transactions, such as those brokered by localbitcoins.com, and does not cover fully on-blockchain transactions that occur outside of a regulated entity, such as trading one cryptocurrency for another.[4] It is also unclear to what extent there is cross-country cooperation in sharing this information, which could be used to deanonymize a large part of unobscured global cryptocurrency usage. This leaves only the more privacy-centric cryptocurrencies.

Even if the anonymous cryptocurrencies are not heavily used, they could be part of a money-laundering chain. Currently, more than 90 percent of total Monero volume is accounted for by currency exchange into or out of bitcoin, although almost all is on a single U.S.-based exchange, which has anti–money laundering reporting requirements. If trading occurs on one of the European exchanges, such as HitBTC, there is regulatory oversight, although the degree of oversight depends on the specific country involved. However, if trading occurs on a decentralized exchange or on one domiciled in a country without regulatory oversight of cryptocurrency (either purposefully or because of a lack of expertise), the transactions could become much harder to trace.

Use in Complementary and Adjacent Markets

Increased use of cryptocurrencies in complementary and adjacent markets could indicate their increased viability among terrorist organizations. Some counterfeiting operations have begun to use darknet markets, and there is a significant trade in stolen credit cards and identities

---

[4] Joy Marie Virga, "International Criminals and Their Virtual Currencies: The Need for an International Effort in Regulating Virtual Currencies and Combating Cyber Crime," *Brazilian Journal of International Law*, Vol. 12, No. 2, 2015.

in these markets.[5] The largest component of these markets, however, is illegal drugs. A recent RAND report looking at darkweb markets notes that "data suggested monthly revenues for international cryptomarkets in double-digit million dollars [in illegal drug sales alone]."[6] This is a very small percentage of the total market for illicit goods, but it does show some signs of adoption of cryptocurrency.

Potentially more worrisome is the combination of illicit uses and more-anonymous currencies, although this adoption is taking some time. Monero was launched in April 2014 and began to be adopted by darkweb markets only in late 2016.[7] The current volume of Monero is unlikely to account for more than a percentage of that, even if the currency were used heavily for that purpose. On the other hand, the price of Monero jumped more than sevenfold in the immediate aftermath of its inclusion in these markets, suggesting that the use was (and is) not insubstantial.[8]

Concerns that Monero, Zcash, or other new technologies have already become "the new cybercrime currency," however, are premature (or misguided).[9] Evidence to date shows that criminals are using these currencies sparsely, if at all—and, in the case of Zcash, the only substantiated criminal use seems to be botnets for mining Zcash.[10]

5   C. Aliens, "Darknet Bust: Global Law Enforcement Raids Massive Counterfeiting Organization," Deep.Dot.Web, December 17, 2016; Lillian Ablon, Martin C. Libicki, and Andrea A. Golay, *Markets for Cybercrime Tools and Stolen Data: Hackers' Bazaar*, Santa Monica, Calif.: RAND Corporation, RR-610-JNI, 2014.

6   Kruithof et al., 2016.

7   Kyle Torpey, "Darknet Customers Are Demanding Bitcoin Alternative Monero," *Bitcoin Magazine*, August 26, 2016.

8   In the weeks after Monero's introduction into the market, the price dropped, although it stabilized at three times its previous value and has climbed more since then. Additionally, the volume climbed by an even larger multiple and remained significantly higher (Coin Market Cap, "Crypto-Currency Market Capitalizations—Monero [XMR]," undated[b]).

9   J. P. Buntinx, "ZCash Becomes the New Cybercrime Currency as Criminals Deploy Malicious Mining Software," themerkle.com, December 15, 2016.

10   A *botnet* refers to a network of private computers infected with malicious software and controlled without the owners' knowledge. Alexander Gostev, "Zcash, or the Return of Malicious Miners," Secure List, blog post, Kaspersky Lab, December 12, 2016.

However, as seen with Monero, darkweb markets take time to incorporate new currencies into their systems. Therefore, although new currencies are not likely to supplant Bitcoin for illicit uses in the short term, it would be surprising if any technology were not used by criminals in various ways eventually.

Factors Decreasing the Viability of Cryptocurrency Use

Continued Infighting Within and Among Cryptocurrencies

Significant uncertainty and infighting have plagued many cryptocurrencies as they grow. To the extent that this leads to uncertainty, it will decrease wider adoption of cryptocurrency, and therefore make cryptocurrency use less viable for terrorist groups. The decentralized nature of governance and management of these currencies makes it difficult for systems to significantly evolve once sufficient diversity exists among users, miners, investors, and other supporters. This has already led to significant infighting, tensions, and blockchain forks in both Bitcoin and Ethereum. These issues have clear negative impacts on the adoption of the technology, especially because the noncryptocurrency alternatives are well understood and stable, with known risks.

It is unclear whether there is a solution that allows for these currencies to be managed without crises that undermine confidence and make the currencies less viable. On the other hand, these are clear problems that are becoming better understood by users and developers, so solutions are being sought. If destabilizing disputes are resolved amicably, even without a clear mechanism for the future, it will provide evidence of some amount of future stability. Otherwise, both industry—which is hesitant to invest in developing the tools and infrastructure to deal with such crises—and regular users who are concerned about the stability and future value of their investments will have less trust in these currencies. That lack of trust discourages terrorist use of cryptocurrencies and slows many of the critical enablers mentioned earlier.

Robust International Regulation and Law Enforcement

Law enforcement cooperation in cybersecurity domains and cryptocurrency markets will be a critical enabler for deanonymization and tracking of funds. In other domains, especially traditional law enforcement, there are multiple options and organizations enabling coordination among regulators and law enforcement personnel. This can be seen in the very widely accepted international crackdowns on child pornography, and, to a lesser extent, in international tracking and prosecution of drug smuggling and money laundering. A critical enabler of this coordination is shared goals. In domains like cybersecurity, there is a complex relationship between countries where intelligence agencies both cooperate and compete, making coordination much harder.

There are a few places where we will see this coordination and cooperation occurring—or not. Fighting darkweb markets provides one useful case study of how this will or will not be done. Multinational cooperation in these new domains requires collaboration between both law enforcement and intelligence, as well as cross-border busts. The channels built for this coordination will both parallel those for CTF and be reused for it.

In a very different way, we will see a clear indication of reduced opportunity for use if these currencies are brought into the regulated financial markets. This would restrict the freedom to transact without providing an identity, but if the freedom of transactions is significantly curtailed, it harms trust in privacy more generally. For this reason, this type of regulation is of great concern to many developers and early backers of cryptocurrency, who view cryptocurrency as a way to evade the shortcomings of traditional financial institutions and state control. The conflict between these groups tilts in favor of regulation as adoption becomes more widespread but will be limited by misalignments or incomplete coordination between countries.

Lastly, there is the possibility of cryptocurrency as an enabler for law enforcement and regulators. Despite cryptocurrency's origins as an antiestablishment alternative, some features make movement in the opposite direction plausible. Exchanges can be explicitly designed for auditing and tracking of funds, and privacy from the public may be preserved while auditability and visibility by regulators are maintained.

Similarly, Zcash, which was designed explicitly for privacy, has features that will allow easier regulatory compliance than either earlier systems or potentially current monetary systems, because the auditing would be built into the protocol. If the systems that are most widely used are incorporated into the regulatory system and those that are incompatible are abandoned or remain marginal because of lack of support, then terrorist groups and other illicit actors may find that the digital world is less, not more, hospitable.

Increasing or Continuing Security Breaches and Hacks of Systems

A series of fraudulent exchanges, theft of improperly secured monies, and similar mishaps have plagued cryptocurrency since it became valuable. Some of these security breaches are arguably because of user error and misplaced trust, but they still serve as evidence to most observers that cryptocurrency is unsafe. Other problems show fundamental weaknesses in normal usage of the system: Unencrypted wallets on internet-connected machines and address reuse are now known to be unfortunate mistakes. If similar issues continue to be discovered and exploited, trust in cryptocurrency systems will remain low.

Conclusion

The utility of cryptocurrencies in the future, as both terrorist methods and cryptocurrencies develop, is unclear. Nonetheless, several recent advances in cryptocurrencies will facilitate their use by the most sophisticated groups that threaten terrorism against Western countries, and the use of cryptocurrencies will be especially enabling for actors that already engage in transnational fundraising and criminal activities. Our research shows that, should a single cryptocurrency emerge that provides widespread adoption, better anonymity, improved security, and that is subject to lax or inconsistent regulation, then the potential utility of this cryptocurrency, as well as the potential for its use by terrorist organizations, would increase. Even if no such currency emerges, there will be some use by terrorist groups, but the extent of that use will depend on the currency's viability. In particular, factors that tend to discourage use include continued instability and infighting in the cryptocurrency community, cooperation between international law enforcement and the intelligence community, and developments in regulation and enforcement.

The indications here provide only a rough guide to how cryptocurrency is most likely to be used, which methods are important to investigate, and which sources of funds are most important to monitor or intercept. As time passes, it will become more obvious how cryptocurrency will and will not be used. As these uncertainties are resolved, terrorist groups will evolve in ways that are unlikely to be fully predictable but will be partially observable over time. The operational challenge of CTF will need to change as well.

CHAPTER SIX

Conclusions

Current concerns about cryptocurrency as a significant enabler of terrorist groups are almost certainly overblown, but coming improvements in cryptocurrency technologies will likely have a significant long-term effect on CTF. The speed at which these technologies are adopted, and the details of which technologies are used and how they are deployed, are critical uncertainties that have important operational impacts. These operational challenges are partly extending current methods of CTF and partly adapting methods from computer security.

Impending change from traditional financial methods to more sophisticated "fintech" (i.e., financial technology) will pose challenges, starting with the addition of new sources to monitor and investigate. This does not necessarily require intentional use by terrorist organizations but simply can be a byproduct of banks changing their practices. For example, the U.S. Treasury "has access to unique financial data about flows of funds within the international financial and commercial system," which is invaluable for tracking illicit flows of money.[1] These sources are potentially imperiled by the trend toward debanking finance via cryptocurrencies, because the adoption of cryptocurrencies might enable secure international fund transfers without needing the current centralized system—perhaps using such cryptocurrency systems as Ripple that exist outside the traditional financial system.

The financial community is historically very conservative, and this has made the tracking of funds a well-understood specialized dis-

---

[1] Zarate, 2013, p. 137.

cipline of forensic accounting. Modern cryptocurrencies are potentially much more flexible, and this may create challenges in financial accounting that look like those involved in attributing and preventing computer intrusions. The field of cryptocurrencies is much less certain, much more dynamic, and one in which innovations might allow terrorist groups to circumvent monitoring. On the other hand, it is a field where sophistication matters; money laundering may be made harder to detect when conducted by sophisticated actors, but many terrorist groups' technical abilities are not currently suited to this type of activity.

Cryptocurrencies: A Short Primer

Bitcoin, which was launched by the pseudonymous Satoshi Nakamoto in early 2009, is both a protocol for securely storing and transmitting tokens (virtual coins) and the name of the unit of value in the system. By 2012, a nascent economy had sprung up around the currency, including exchanges to and from traditional fiat currencies and the darknet market Silk Road. The various licit and illicit uses for bitcoin (as well as speculation) led to a significant increase in the price and a variety of news stories that brought Bitcoin into the public eye.

Simultaneously, a series of alternate cryptocurrencies was launched with varying levels of success, many of which have been near-clones of Bitcoin. Such so-called "altcoins" have generally had only minor modifications from Bitcoin's technical and operational parameters.[1]

Bitcoin

In brief, Bitcoin can be understood as revolving around a public ledger called the *blockchain*, which is maintained by an online distributed network of computers that track transactions and maintain a complete history of verified transactions.[2] Bitcoin is "distributed" in that anyone

---

[1]   Such parameters include the frequency of rewards, number of coins generated, and cryptographic systems and related cryptographic parameters used.

[2]   For a technical explanation of Bitcoin and related currencies, see Andreas M. Antonopoulos, *Mastering Bitcoin: Programming the Open Blockchain*, Sebastopol, Calif.: O'Reilly Media, Inc., 2017; and Arvind Narayanan, Joseph Bonneau, Edward W. Felten, Andrew Miller, and

can participate in all aspects of its operations, including all transactions, but no single participant has control. Anyone with an internet connection can view or submit new transactions to the public ledger. These new transactions are then validated and appended by the distributed network; the validation process occurs in groups, or "blocks," of transactions, and the process of appending them is the "chaining" operation referenced in the name "blockchain."

One of the central challenges for a digital currency for which Bitcoin has provided a solution is maintaining the anonymity of transaction participants while unambiguously and securely proving ownership of transacted funds. In order for Bitcoin to support anonymity and transaction ownership, transaction participants are identified by a unique string of random numbers rather than by a name or other personal information. This anonymity is weak because, although the string of numbers is random, if that string is used multiple times as an identity, it can be used to track transactions over time and correlate people to the random identifiers they use. As a result, the Bitcoin Foundation recommends that users change their identifying string with each new transaction, which is done by default by most Bitcoin clients today. (The random string that identifies users has a second important purpose: It constitutes the mechanism by which participants prove their anonymous ownership over the currency.)[3]

As discussed in an earlier RAND report, it is worth stressing that a user does not own bitcoins.[4] Rather, a user has the right to spend bitcoins associated with addresses and private keys. The private keys,

---

Steven Goldfeder, *Bitcoin and Cryptocurrency Technologies: A Comprehensive Introduction*, Princeton, N.J.: Princeton University Press, 2016.

[3] More technically, the random string that identifies every user is a unique public key of a digital signature scheme. A digital signature scheme is a cryptographic means by which users can prove that they were the authors of digital information; there is a public key that identifies the user and is published for all to see and a private key that the user keeps secret. Bitcoin uses this mechanism to prove ownership: Because the identity of each user in a transaction is that user's public key, the payer can prove ownership of the bitcoins she owns by signing the transaction with her secret key. Because her identity is her public key, anyone who views the transaction can verify this.

[4] Baron et al., 2015.

in aggregate, are referred to as a bitcoin "wallet," and this collection of keys can be used to transact the bitcoins associated with addresses.[5] Accordingly, a bitcoin wallet is actually the requisite information proving ownership of bitcoins. The addresses themselves are based on a public/private key pair that is generated cryptographically. The private key allows the coins to be spent in a new transaction. It is conceptually similar to having an address with a locked mailbox: Anyone can deliver mail, but only someone with the key can take letters out and send them to a new address, thereby transferring or spending them. In this case, no one necessarily knows who has the key, and the mailboxes are on the blockchain.

Mining is the process by which transactions are irreversibly locked into the blockchain so that transactions cannot be altered later. At a very high level, those who participate in the mining process— miners—compete to find the solution to a very difficult cryptographic function, called a "hash function." Anyone with a computer can be a miner, although miners with more-powerful computers are able to find the solution more quickly than others. Importantly, the miner who finds the solution to the problem simultaneously validates and locks into place the set of all previous bitcoin transactions thus far. The reason that a miner wants to find such a solution is that he or she is rewarded with new bitcoin (hence the mining terminology). Two important takeaways of the mining process are: (1) Bitcoin is secure because it incentivizes people to secure it through the mining process, and (2) anyone who can sufficiently subvert the mining process can subvert the security of Bitcoin.[6]

---

[5]   More-complex transaction types allow a group of different keys to sign a single transaction together, with many inputs and many outputs. This can allow a single person to spend multiple previous outputs, multiple people to pay for something together, or multiple people to "mix" their bitcoins, making it unclear which input was sent to which output, providing additional privacy. Other complex transactions are possible, such as outputting the bitcoin to any account fulfilling some condition, requiring multiple distinct keys to spend the outputs, or locking the money for some period of time, but these transactions are less widely used. Some later cryptocurrencies (other than Bitcoin and its clones) have additional transaction types and capabilities.

[6]   There have been notable examples of bitcoins being stolen through hacking, but more recently, bitcoins have been stolen through a variety of attacks that subvert the mining pro-

Cryptocurrencies Other Than Bitcoin

By the end of 2013, it was clear that, although Bitcoin was becoming a more valuable system, most near-clone "altcoins" had little of value to offer as an alternative. New cryptocurrencies that were launched needed a clearer value proposition, and two significant alternatives were pursued: a series of significantly different uses for blockchain technology, many of which were less exclusively about currency, and newer cryptocurrencies with more-specific value propositions. Given the importance of illicit activities for the rise of Bitcoin, it is unsurprising that many of these newer cryptocurrencies enabled more flexibility for commerce and transactions, more privacy, or both.

This group of altcoins included Omni Layer (MasterCoin), BlackCoin, and Monero.[7] They were touted as more private and secure but were therefore seemingly tailor-made for illicit activities that were already becoming a popular use for Bitcoin. Each has various features that enable illicit uses, such as privacy enhancing stealth addresses and transaction mixing,[8] and assistance for illicit transactions such as built-in second-party escrow for transactions with untrusted third parties.[9] Some of these innovations provide privacy protection that fundamentally changes the transparency around transactions that exist in Bitcoin without sacrificing their verifiability by the use of more-complex cryptographic mechanisms. At the time of this writing, the most popular of these is Monero. One of Bitcoin's drawbacks is that users have a single pseudonymous identity that they then have to change, ideally after each transaction. By contrast, Monero uses special types of cryp-

---

cess itself. See, for example, New Sky Security, "Cryptocurrency Mining Hacks: How Thefts Steal Bitcoin and Ethereum," Medium blog post, April 24, 2018.

[7]   See "Omni Layer," homepage, undated; "BlackCoin," homepage, undated; and "Monero. How," homepage, undated.

[8]   Bitcoin transactions from multiple, unrelated participants can be "mixed" prior to posting to the public ledger, which provides additional security by hiding the transaction amounts and the partners to the transactions.

[9]   Built-in second-party escrow services provide an intermediary who "holds" the bitcoins until each party to the transaction has notified the second party that the contract terms are satisfied, similar to the way real estate escrow companies hold deposits prior to closing.

tographic mechanisms called "ring signatures" that enable pseudonym reuse while making it more difficult to associate a pseudonym with a user spending money and "stealth addresses" that hide the recipient.[10]

Zcash represents a significant technical departure from previous cryptocurrencies. Launched in October 2016, Zcash allows transactions to transfer money held outside of the visible blockchain, so that transactions are no longer identified by an owner at all. This private mode of transaction is viewable only to the originator and those possessing a "view key" for the individual transaction, which allows them to see specific private transactions without revealing the user's private key used to create the hidden transactions. Zcash is able to accomplish these advances through the use of Zero Knowledge Succinct Arguments of Knowledge (ZK-SnARKs). On the other hand, weaknesses in the system or the implementation could, in theory, allow different classes of attacks than those that apply to other systems.[11] Additionally, the entire protocol is based on much more complex cryptographic setups and assumptions than earlier systems.[12] Ultimately, Zcash provides the potential ability to use and transfer the currency offline, which could make it difficult or impossible for an external watcher (such as law enforcement) to trace illicit transactions.

---

[10] More technically, ring signatures are when transactions are signed by one member of a group, but which member signed it cannot be determined. Thus, Monero allows individuals to maintain anonymity by making it difficult for someone watching the transaction to know whom it was by; not only is it unclear who the owner of the funds is, but it is also unclear which fund owner was the one who engaged in the transaction. Stealth addresses allow a recipient to determine that they received money to a new address using their existing private key without the spender revealing the corresponding public key.

[11] No such weaknesses have been uncovered, and this is currently a purely theoretical concern. However, Zcash is a new and complex system, both of which make flaws harder for developers to notice and unlikely to be discovered quickly. The zero-knowledge methods used are very novel, and although the system has been developed and then vetted by leading cryptographers, similarly vetted and much less complex cryptographic systems often have had vulnerabilities uncovered years later.

[12] These include the Common Reference String setup assumption and nonfalsifiable hardness assumptions. The drawbacks of relying on these assumptions are unclear; generally speaking, the more complex a cryptographic systems is, the more risky the setup.

Other cryptocurrencies and systems that employ the blockchain ledger technology that would allow similar capabilities are in development. Hawk is one proposed means of allowing fully private contracts and transactions on the Ethereum blockchain, which, among other new features, would allow users to engage in Zcash-like transactions where the users, amounts, and other details can be hidden.[13] A different model for this is "ZCash over Ethereum," which implements the Zcash protocol using Ethereum contracts, independent of the Zcash blockchain.

---

[13] Ahmed Kosba, Andrew Miller, Elaine Shi, Zikai Wen, and Charalampos Papamanthou "Hawk: The Blockchain Model of Cryptography and Privacy-Preserving Smart Contracts," San Jose, Calif.: Institute of Electrical and Electronics Engineers Symposium on Security and Privacy 2016, May 22–26, 2016.

Bibliography

Abboushi, Suhail, "Global Virtual Currency—Brief Overview," *Journal of Applied Business and Economics*, Vol. 19, No. 6, 2017, pp. 10–18.

Ablon, Lillian, Martin C. Libicki, and Andrea A. Golay, *Markets for Cybercrime Tools and Stolen Data: Hackers' Bazaar*, Santa Monica, Calif.: RAND Corporation, RR-610-JNI, 2014. As of December 27, 2016:
http://www.rand.org/pubs/research_reports/RR610.html

Acharya, Arabinda, *Targeting Terrorist Financing: International Cooperation and New Regimes*, New York: Routledge, 2009.

Ali, Syed Taha, Patrick McCorry, Peter Hyun-Jeen Lee, and Feng Hao, "ZombieCoin: Powering Next-Generation Botnets with Bitcoin," paper presented at the 19th International Conference on Financial Cryptography and Data Security 2015, San Jose, Puerto Rico, January 26–30, 2015.

Aliens, C., "Darknet Bust: Global Law Enforcement Raids Massive Counterfeiting Organization," Deep.Dot.Web, December 17, 2016. As of February 22, 2019:
https://www.deepdotweb.com/2016/12/17/darknet-bust-global-law-enforcement-raids-massive-counterfeiting-organization

al-Munthir, Taqi'ul-Deen, "Bitcoin wa Sadaqat al-Jihad: Bitcoin and the Charity of Violent Physical Struggle," self-published article, August 2014. As of March 5, 2019:
https://krypt3ia.files.wordpress.com/2014/07/btcedit-21.pdf

Altcoins, homepage, undated. As of February 24, 2015:
http://altcoins.com

Andreessen, Marc, "Why Bitcoin Matters," *New York Times*, January 21, 2014. As of February 23, 2015:
http://dealbook.nytimes.com/2014/01/21/why-bitcoin-matters

Andrychowicz, Marcin, Stefan Dziembowski, Daniel Malinowski, and Łukasz Mazurek, "Secure Multiparty Computations on Bitcoin," paper presented at the Institute of Electrical and Electronics Engineers Symposium on Security and Privacy, San Jose, Calif., May 18–21, 2014.

Antonopoulos, Andreas M., *Mastering Bitcoin: Programming the Open Blockchain*, Sebastopol, Calif.: O'Reilly Media, Inc., 2017.

Apostolaki, Maria, Aviv Zohar, and Laurent Vanbever, "Hijacking Bitcoin: Large-Scale Network Attacks on Cryptocurrencies," Arxiv.org, May 2016. As of December 29, 2016:
https://btc-hijack.ethz.ch/files/btc_hijack.pdf

Apple, "Touch ID Security. Right at Your Fingertips," webpage, undated.

Atlas, Kristov, "Weak Privacy Guarantees for SharedCoin Mixing Service," security advisory blog post, June 9, 2014a. As of February 21, 2019:
http://www.coinjoinsudoku.com/advisory/

———, "An Analysis of Darkcoin's Blockchain Privacy via Darksend+," self-published article, September 19, 2014b. As of July 6, 2016:
http://cdn.anonymousbitcoinbook.com/darkcoin/darksend-paper/Atlas_Darksend-Analysis-v001.pdf

———, *Anonymous Bitcoin: How to Keep Your [Bitcoin] All to Yourself*, self-published, 2015.

Auroracoin, "Why Iceland? Many Governments Have Abused Their National Currencies, but Why Is Iceland Such a Good Place for the First National Cryptocurrency?" undated.

Baron, Joshua, Angela O'Mahony, David Manheim, and Cynthia Dion-Schwarz, *National Security Implications of Virtual Currencies: Examining the Potential for Non-state Actor Deployment*, Santa Monica, Calif.: RAND Corporation, RR-1231-OSD, 2015. As of June 15, 2018:
https://www.rand.org/pubs/research_reports/RR1231.html

Barotseland Free State, *Barotseland Mupu Currency Act of 2012*, February 28, 2012. As of April 16, 2015:
http://www.barotseland.info/Currency_Act.htm

Ben-Sasson, Eli, Alessandro Chiesa, Christina Garman, Matthew Green, Ian Miers, Eran Tromer, and Madars Virza, "SNARKs for C: Verifying Program Executions Succinctly and in Zero Knowledge," in Ram Canetti and Juan A. Garay, eds., *Advances in Cryptology—CRYPTO 2013: 33rd Annual Cryptology Conference*, Santa Barbara, Calif., August 2013, pp. 90–108.

———, "Zerocash: Decentralized Anonymous Payments from Bitcoin," paper presented at the 2014 Institute of Electrical and Electronics Engineers Symposium on Security and Privacy, San Jose, Calif., May 18–21, 2014a.

———, "Zerocash: Decentralized Anonymous Payments from Bitcoin," extended version of the paper presented at the 2014 Institute of Electrical and Electronics Engineers Symposium on Security and Privacy, San Jose, Calif., May 18–21, 2014b. As of February 20, 2015:
http://zerocash-project.org/media/pdf/zerocash-extended-20140518.pdf

Berman, Eli, *Radical, Religious, and Violent: The New Economics of Terrorism*, Cambridge, Mass.: MIT Press, 2009.

Bernstein, Peter L., *The Power of Gold: The History of an Obsession*, Hoboken, N.J.: Wiley and Sons, Inc., 2004.

Biryukov, Alex, and Ivan Pustogarov, "Bitcoin over Tor Isn't a Good Idea," paper presented at the 2015 Institute of Electrical and Electronics Engineers Symposium on Security and Privacy, San Jose, Calif., May 18–20, 2015a.

———, "Proof-of-Work as Anonymous Micropayment: Rewarding a Tor Relay," paper presented at the 19th International Conference on Financial Cryptography and Data Security 2015, San Jose, Puerto Rico, January 26–30, 2015b.

Bit Clone, homepage, undated. As of February 24, 2015:
http://www.bitclone.net/

Bitcoin, "Choose Your Bitcoin Wallet," webpage, undated(a). As of February 19, 2015:
https://bitcoin.org/en/choose-your-wallet

———, "Protect Your Privacy," webpage, undated(b). As of February 22, 2015:
https://bitcoin.org/en/protect-your-privacy

———, "Some Things You Need to Know," webpage, undated(c). As of February 20, 2015:
https://bitcoin.org/en/you-need-to-know

"Bitcoin ATM Location Profile," coinlocations.com, undated. As of March 1, 2018:
https://coinlocations.com/
bitcoin-atm-locations-map-find-your-nearest-bitcoin-atm-location/
profile/a:bitcoin-atm-machine-in-jubail-at-ticket-computer-center---lamassu

Bitcoin Forum, "[RELEASE] Liquidcoin (Speculation Based)," discussion thread begun January 18, 2012. As of February 26, 2015:
https://bitcointalk.org/index.php?topic=60026.0

———, "CoinJoin: Bitcoin Privacy for the Real World," discussion thread begun August 22, 2013. As of February 22, 2015:
https://bitcointalk.org/index.php?topic=279249.0

Bitcoin Help, homepage, undated. As of February 25, 2015:
https://bitcoinhelp.net/

Bitcoin Wiki, "Comparison of Cryptocurrencies," webpage, December 24, 2014. As of February 24, 2015:
https://en.bitcoin.it/wiki/Comparison_of_cryptocurrencies

———, "Hardware Wallet," webpage, August 15, 2015a. As of February 19, 2015:
https://en.bitcoin.it/wiki/Hardware_wallet

————, homepage, August 13, 2015b. As of February 25, 2015:
https://en.bitcoin.it/wiki/Main_Page

————, "Mining Hardware Comparison," webpage, September 16, 2015c. As June 25, 2015:
https://en.bitcoin.it/wiki/Mining_hardware_comparison

————, "Weaknesses," webpage, July 8, 2015d. As of February 16, 2015:
https://en.bitcoin.it/wiki/Weaknesses

Bitsim, homepage, undated. As of April 28, 2015:
https://www.bitsim.com/en/

"BlackCoin," homepage, undated. As of January 20, 2018:
https://blackcoin.org/

Blanc, Jerome, "Thirty Years of Community and Complementary Currencies," *International Journal of Community Currency Research*, Vol. 16, 2012, pp. D1–4.

Blockchain, homepage, undated(a). As of June 25, 2015:
https://blockchain.info

————, "Market Capitalization," webpage, undated(b). As of February 19, 2015:
https://blockchain.info/charts/market-cap?timespan=all&showDataPoints=false&daysAverageString=1&show_header=true&scale=0&address

————, "Tutorial: How to Send Bitcoins Using Email or SMS Messages," webpage, undated(c). As of March 5, 2015:
https://blog.blockchain.com/2014/08/26/tutorial-how-to-send-bitcoins-using-email-or-sms-messages/

Bowe, Sean, "zkSNARKs in Ethereum," Zcash blog, July 28, 2016. As of February 22, 2019:
https://z.cash/blog/zksnarks-in-ethereum.html

Bonneau, Joseph, Andrew Miller, Jeremy Clark, Arvind Narayanan, Joshua A. Kroll, and Edward W. Felten, "Research Perspectives on Bitcoin and Second-Generation Cryptocurrencies," *Proceedings of IEEE Security and Privacy 2015*, San Jose, Calif.: Institute of Electrical and Electronics Engineers Computer Society, May 2015.

Bonneau, Joseph, Arvind Narayanan, Andrew Miller, Jeremy Clark, and Joshua A. Kroll, "Mixcoin: Anonymity for Bitcoin with Accountable Mixes," *Financial Cryptography and Data Security 2014*, 2014.

Brantly, Aaron, "Financing Terror Bit by Bit," *CTC Sentinel*, Vol. 7, No. 10, October 2014, pp. 1–5.

Brill, Alan, and Lonnie Keene, "Cryptocurrencies: The Next Generation of Terrorist Financing?" *Defence Against Terrorism Review*, Vol. 6, No. 1, 2014, pp. 7–30.

Brown, Steven David, "Cryptocurrency and Criminality: The Bitcoin Opportunity," *Police Journal: Theory, Practice and Principles*, Vol. 89, No. 4, December 2016, pp. 327–339.

Buntinx, J. P., "ZCash Becomes the New Cybercrime Currency as Criminals Deploy Malicious Mining Software," themerkle.com, December 15, 2016. As of February 22, 2019:
http://themerkle.com/zcash-becomes-the-new-cybercrime-currency-as-criminals-deploy-malicious-mining-software/

Buterin, Vitalik, *A Next Generation Smart Contract & Decentralized Application Platform*, Ethereum White Paper, 2015. As of March 1, 2019:
https://pdfs.semanticscholar.org/0dbb/8a54ca5066b82fa086bbf5db4c54b947719a.pdf?_ga=2.89019099.1392279181.1551472600-925499253.1551038223

Byman, Daniel L., "How to Hunt a Lone Wolf: Countering Terrorists Who Act on Their Own," op-ed, Washington, D.C.: Brookings Institution, February 14, 2017. As of February 13, 2019:
https://www.brookings.edu/opinions/
how-to-hunt-a-lone-wolf-countering-terrorists-who-act-on-their-own/

Callimachi, Rukmini, "Not 'Lone Wolves' After All: How ISIS Guides World's Terror Plots from Afar," *New York Times*, February 4, 2017. As of June 20, 2017:
https://www.nytimes.com/2017/02/04/world/asia/
isis-messaging-app-terror-plot.html

Carmona, Anais, "The Bitcoin: The Currency of the Future, Fuel of Terror," in Misty Blowers, ed., *Evolution of Cyber Technologies and Operations to 2035*, Switzerland: Springer International Publishing, 2015, pp. 127–135.

Chaum, David, "Blind Signatures for Untraceable Payments," in David Chaum, Ronald L. Rivest, and Alan T. Sherman, eds., *Advances in Cryptology: Proceedings of Crypto '82*, Berlin: Springer-Verlag, 1983, pp. 199–203.

Chaum, David, Amos Fiat, and Moni Naor, "Untraceable Electronic Cash," in Shafi Goldwasser, ed., *Advances in Cryptology: Proceedings of Crypto '88*, Berlin: Springer-Verlag, 1990, pp. 319–327.

Christin, Nicolas, "Traveling the Silk Road: A Measurement Analysis of a Large Anonymous Online Marketplace," *Proceedings of the 22nd International Conference on World Wide Web (WWW 2013)*, Rio de Janeiro: World Wide Web Conference, 2013, pp. 213–223.

Clarke, Colin P., *Terrorism, Inc.: The Financing of Terrorism, Insurgency, and Irregular Warfare*, Santa Barbara, Calif.: Praeger Security International, 2015.

Code of Federal Regulations, Title 31, Money and Finance: Treasury; Subtitle B, Regulations Relating to Money and Finance; Subchapter X, Financial Crimes Enforcement Network, Department of the Treasury; Parts 1010, 1021, and 1022, Bank Secrecy Act Regulations; Definitions and Other Regulations Relating to Money Services Businesses. As of February 21, 2019:
https://www.gpo.gov/fdsys/pkg/FR-2011-07-21/pdf/2011-18309.pdf

Cohen, Benjamin J., *The Geography of Money*, Ithaca, N.Y.: Cornell University Press, 1998.

Coin Creator, homepage, undated. As of February 24, 2015:
http://coincreator.net/

CoinJoin, "Weaknesses in SharedCoin," undated. As of February 22, 2015:
http://www.coinjoinsudoku.com

Coin Market Cap, "Crypto-Currency Market Capitalizations—Dogecoin (DOGE)," webpage, undated(a). As of February 26, 2015:
https://coinmarketcap.com/currencies/dogecoin/

———, "Crypto-Currency Market Capitalizations—Monero (XMR)," webpage, undated(b). As of February 22, 2019:
https://coinmarketcap.com/currencies/monero/

———, "Crypto-Currency Market Capitalizations," webpage, September 30, 2015. As of June 25, 2015:
https://coinmarketcap.com

Cointelegraph Media Partners, "Map of Coins," homepage, undated. As of February 16, 2015:
http://mapofcoins.com/

Covert, Adrian, "There's a Virus That Will Steal All Your Bitcoins," Gizmodo.com, June 17, 2011. As of February 25, 2015:
http://gizmodo.com/5813039/theres-a-virus-that-will-steal-all-your-bitcoins

Cragin, Kim, Peter Chalk, Sara A. Daly, Brian A. Jackson, *Sharing the Dragon's Teeth: Terrorist Groups and the Exchange of New Technologies*, Santa Monica, Calif.: RAND Corporation, MG-485-DHS, 2007. As of February 21, 2019:
https://www.rand.org/pubs/monographs/MG485.html

Cuperman, Miron (devrandom), and Chris Taylor, "The Problem with Bitcoin Hardware Wallets (and possible solutions)" GitHub draft, March 9, 2014. As of February 21, 2019:
https://github.com/devrandom/btc-papers/blob/master/hardware-wallet-security.md

Daftari, Lisa, "Hezbollah's New Crowdfunding Campaign: 'Equip a Mujahid,'" Foreign Desk, February 9, 2017. As of February 21, 2019:
http://www.foreigndesknews.com/world/middle-east/hezbollahs-new-crowdfunding-campaign-equip-mujahid

Danezis, George, Cédric Fournet, Markulf Kohlweiss, and Bryan Parno, "Pinocchio Coin: Building Zerocoin from a Succinct Pairing-Based Proof System," *PETShop '13: Proceedings of the First ACM Workshop on Language Support for Privacy-Enhancing Technologies*, New York: Association for Computing Machinery, 2013, pp. 27–30.

Daragahi, Borzo, "ISIS Declares Its Own Currency," *Financial Times* online, November 13, 2014. As of February 24, 2015:
https://www.ft.com/content/
baf893e0-6b4f-11e4-9337-00144feabdc0#axzz3SgRLthZp

Dark Wallet, homepage, undated. As of February 22, 2015:
https://www.darkwallet.is

Dash, homepage, undated(a). As of March 5, 2019:
https://www.dash.org/

———, "Understanding Masternodes," webpage, 2018. As of March 5, 2019:
https://docs.dash.org/en/stable/masternodes/understanding.html

Dash Forum, "Reply to Kristov's Paper," self-published article, September 11, 2014. As of March 5, 2019:
https://www.dash.org/forum/threads/reply-to-kristovs-paper.2325

Davies, Glyn, *A History of Money: From Ancient Times to the Present Day*, Chicago: University of Chicago Press, 2005.

Defense Advanced Research Projects Agency, "DARPA Demo Day 2014 Highlights Innovative Approaches to Preserving and Expanding U.S. Technological Superiority," press release, May 21, 2014. As of March 5, 2019:
https://www.darpa.mil/news-events/2014-05-21

Defense Science Board, U.S. Department of Defense, *Task Force Report: Resilient Military Systems and the Advanced Cyber Threat*, January 2013. As of March 5, 2019:
https://nsarchive2.gwu.edu/NSAEBB/NSAEBB424/docs/Cyber-081.pdf

Desan, Christine, *Making Money: Coin, Currency, and the Coming of Capitalism*, Oxford: Oxford University Press, 2014.

Directorate General for Internal Policies, Policy Department for Citizens' Rights and Constitutional Affairs, *Virtual Currencies and Terrorist Financing: Assessing the Risks and Evaluating Responses*, Brussels: European Parliament, 2018, p. 9. As of March 1, 2019:
http://www.europarl.europa.eu/RegData/etudes/STUD/2018/604970/
IPOL_STU(2018)604970_EN.pdf

Dowd, Kevin, "Contemporary Private Monetary Systems," self-published paper, August 2013. As of February 26, 2015:
http://www.kevindowd.org/app/download/8477462997/
Contemporary+Private+Monetary+Systems.pdf ?t=1380159881

D'Souza, Jayesh, *Terrorist Financing, Money Laundering, and Tax Evasion: Examining the Performance of Financial Intelligence Units*, New York: CRC Press, Taylor and Francis Group, 2012.

El Defrawy, Karim, and Joshua Lampkins, "Founding Digital Currency on Secure Computation," *CCS '14: Proceedings of ACM SIGSAC Conference on Computer and Communications Security*, March 2014, pp. 1–14.

Ensafi, Roya, Philipp Winter, Abdullah Mueen, and Jedidiah R. Crandall, "Large-Scale Spatiotemporal Characterization of Inconsistencies in the World's Largest Firewall," self-published paper, October 3, 2014. As of February 22, 2015: http://arxiv.org/pdf/1410.0735.pdf

European Banking Authority, "EBA Opinion on 'Virtual Currencies,'" July 4, 2014. As of March 5, 2019: https://eba.europa.eu/documents/%2010180/657547/ EBA-Op-2014-08+Opinion+on+Virtual+Currencies.pdf

European Central Bank, *Virtual Currency Schemes*, Frankfurt, October 2012. As of October 1, 2015: https://www.ecb.europa.eu/pub/pdf/other/virtualcurrencyschemes201210en.pdf

Eyal, Ittay, and Emin Gun Sirer, "Majority Is Not Enough: Bitcoin Mining Is Vulnerable," in Nicolas Christin and Reihaneh Safavi-Naini, eds., *Financial Cryptography and Data Security: 18th International Conference*, FC 2014, March 2014, pp. 436–454.

FATF—*See* Financial Action Task Force.

Federal Bureau of Investigation, "Ransomware on the Rise: FBI and Partners Working to Combat This Cyber Threat," webpage, January 20, 2015. As of February 13, 2015: http://www.fbi.gov/news/stories/2015/january/ransomware-on-the-rise

Financial Action Task Force, *Emerging Terrorist Financing Risks*, Paris: Financial Action Task Force and the Organisation for Economic Co-operation and Development, October 2015. As of February 21, 2019: http://www.fatf-gafi.org/media/fatf/documents/reports/ Emerging-Terrorist-Financing-Risks.pdf

Folding Coin, "Announcing Scotcoin," webpage, February 5, 2015. As of February 21, 2019: https://foldingcoin.net/index.php/news/263-news-announcing-scotcoin

Freeman, Michael, and Moyara Ruehsen, "Terrorism Financing Methods: An Overview," *Perspectives on Terrorism*, Vol. 7, No. 4, August 2013.

Frieden, Jeffry A., *Global Capitalism: Its Fall and Rise in the Twentieth Century*, New York: W. W. Norton and Company, 2006.

Garay, Juan, Aggelos Kiayias, and Nikos Leonardos, "The Bitcoin Backbone Protocol: Analysis and Applications," in Elisabeth Oswald and Marc Fischlin, eds., *Advances in Cryptology—EUROCRYPT 2015: 34th Annual International Conference on the Theory and Applications of Crypotgraphic Techniques*, April 2015, pp. 281–310.

Giechaskiel, Ilias, Cas Cremers, and Kasper B. Rasmussen, "On Bitcoin Security in the Presence of Broken Cryptographic Primitives," Heraklion, Greece: 21st European Symposium on Research in Computer Security, September 26–30, 2016, pp. 201–222.

Gill, Nathan, "Ecuador Turning to Virtual Currency After Oil Loans," Bloomberg News, August 11, 2014. As of March 5, 2019:
https://www.bloomberg.com/news/articles/2014-08-11/
ecuador-turning-to-virtual-currency-after-oil-loans-correct-

GitHub, "Omni Protocol Specification (formerly Mastercoin)," undated. As of February 26, 2015:
https://github.com/OmniLayer/spec

Goldman, Zachary K., Ellie Maruyama, Elizabeth Rosenberg, Edoardo Saravalle, and Julia Solomon-Strauss, *Terrorist Use of Virtual Currencies: Containing the Potential Threat*, Washington, D.C.: Center for a New American Security, May 2017.

Gomez, Georgina, "Sustainability of the Argentine Complementary Currency Systems: Four Governance Systems," *International Journal of Community Currency Research*, Vol. 16, 2012, pp. D80–89.

Gosler, James R., and Lewis Von Thaer, *Task Force Report: Resilient Military Systems and the Advanced Cyber Threat*, Washington, D.C.: Defense Science Board, U.S. Department of Defense, January 2013.

Gostev, Alexander, "Zcash, or the Return of Malicious Miners," Secure List, blog post, Kaspersky Lab, December 12, 2016. As of February 22, 2019:
https://securelist.com/blog/research/76862/
zcash-or-the-return-of-malicious-miners/

Greenberg, Andy, "Hacker Redirects Traffic from 19 Internet Providers to Steal Bitcoin," *Wired*, August 7, 2014. As of December 29, 2016:
https://www.wired.com/2014/08/isp-bitcoin-theft/

———, "Monero, the Drug Dealer's Cryptocurrency of Choice, Is on Fire," *Wired*, January 25, 2017. As of February 22, 2019:
https://www.wired.com/2017/01/monero-drug-dealers-cryptocurrency-choice-fire/

Hales, Thomas C., "The NSA Back Door to NIST," *Notices of the AMS*, Vol. 61, No. 2, February 2014, pp. 190–192.

Heilman, Ethan, Leen AlShenibr, Foteini Baldimtsi, Alessandra Scafuro, and Sharon Goldberg, "TumbleBit: An Untrusted Bitcoin-Compatible Anonymous Payment Hub," International Association for Cryptologic Research, 2016. As of February 21, 2019:
https://eprint.iacr.org/2016/575.pdf

Helleiner, Eric, *The Making of National Money: Territorial Currencies in Historical Perspective*, Ithaca, N.Y.: Cornell University Press, 2003.

Hruska, Joel, "One Bitcoin Group Now Controls 51% of Total Mining Power, Threatening Entire Currency's Safety," Exteremtech.com, June 16, 2014. As of February 21, 2019:
https://www.extremetech.com/extreme/184427-one-bitcoin-group-now-controls-51-of-total-mining-power-threatening-entire-currencys-safety

Hudson, Rex, *Terrorist and Organized Crime Groups in the Tri-Border Area (TBA) of South America*, Washington, D.C.: Library of Congress, Federal Research Division, 2003. As of February 21, 2019:
https://www.loc.gov/rr/frd/pdf-files/TerrOrgCrime_TBA.pdf

Irish Coin, homepage, undated.

Ithaca HOURS, homepage, undated. As of February 24, 2015:
http://www.ithacahours.com/

Jack, William, and Tavneet Suri, "Mobile Money: The Economics of M-Pesa," National Bureau of Economic Research, Working Paper No. 16721, January 2011. As of March 5, 2019:
https://www.nber.org/papers/w16721

Johnson, Marion, "The Cowrie Currencies of West Africa. Part I," *Journal of African History*, Vol. 11, No. 1, 1970, pp. 17–49.

Johnston, Patrick B., Jacob N. Shapiro, Howard J. Shatz, Benjamin Bahney, Danielle F. Jung, Patrick K. Ryan, and Jonathan Wallace, *Foundations of the Islamic State: Management, Money, and Terror in Iraq, 2005–2010*, Santa Monica, Calif.: RAND Corporation, RR-1192-DARPA, 2016. As of February 20, 2019:
https://www.rand.org/pubs/research_reports/RR1192.html

Jones, Seth G., and Patrick B. Johnston, "The Future of Insurgency," *Studies In Conflict and Terrorism*, Vol. 36, No. 1, 2013, pp. 1–25.

Kaelberer, Matthias, "Trust in the Euro: Exploring the Governance of a Supra-National Currency," *European Societies*, Vol. 9, No. 4, 2007, pp. 623–642.

Kharif, Olga, "Bitcoin: Not Just for Libertarians and Anarchists Anymore," Bloomberg Business, October 9, 2014.

Kimhy, Eliad, "NotPetya Intrusion Vectors and Propagation," Cybereason Intelligence Team, June 30, 2017. As of February 21, 2019:
https://www.cybereason.com/notpetya-intrusion-vectors-and-propagation/

Kindleberger, Charles, *A Financial History of Western Europe*, Oxford, UK: Oxford University Press, 1993.

King, Sunny, "Primecoin: Cryptocurrency with Prime Number Proof-of-Work," self-published paper, July 7, 2013. As of February 19, 2015: http://primecoin.io/bin/primecoin-paper.pdf

King, Sunny, and Scott Nadal, "PPCoin: Peer-to-Peer Crypto-Currency with Proof-of-Stake," self-published paper, August 19, 2012. As of February 24, 2015: http://archive.org/stream/PPCoinPaper/ppcoin-paper_djvu.txt

Kosba, Ahmed, Andrew Miller, Elaine Shi, Zikai Wen, and Charalampos Papamanthou "Hawk: The Blockchain Model of Cryptography and Privacy-Preserving Smart Contracts," San Jose, Calif.: Institute of Electrical and Electronics Engineers Symposium on Security and Privacy 2016, May 22–26, 2016, pp. 839–858.

Krebs, Brian, "True Goodbye: 'Using TrueCrypt Is Not Secure,'" KrebsonSecurity. com, May 14, 2014. As of February 19, 2015: http://www.krebsonsecurity.com/2014/05/ true-goodbye-using-truecrypt-is-not-secure/

———, "U.S. Government Seizes LibertyReserve.com," KrebsonSecurity.com, May 13, 2013. As of March 5, 2019: https://krebsonsecurity.com/2013/05/ u-s-government-seizes-libertyreserve-com/

Kroll, Joshua A., Ian C. Davey, and Edward W. Felten, "The Economics of Bitcoin Mining or, Bitcoin in the Presence of Adversaries," paper presented at the 12th Workshop on the Economics of Information Security (WEIS 2013), Washington, D.C., June 11–12, 2013.

Krombholz, Katharina, Aljosha Judmayer, Matthias Gusenbauer, and Edgar Weippl, "The Other Side of the Coin: User Experiences with Bitcoin Security and Privacy," Financial Cryptography and Data Security 2016 Conference, Barbados, February 22–26, 2016. As of February 21, 2019: https://www.sba-research.org/wp-content/uploads/publications/ TheOtherSideOfTheCoin_FC16preConf.pdf

Kruithof, Kristy, Judith Aldridge, David Décary Hétu, Megan Sim, Elma Dujso, and Stijn Hoorens, *Internet-Facilitated Drugs Trade: An Analysis of the Size, Scope and the Role of the Netherlands*, Santa Monica, Calif.: RAND Corporation, RR-1607-WODC, 2016. As of February 21, 2019: https://www.rand.org/pubs/research_reports/RR1607.html

Kuhn, Richard D., Vincent C. Hu, W. Timothy Polk, and Shu-Jen Chang, *Introduction to Public Key Technology and the Federal PKI Infrastructure*, Gaithersburg, Md.: National Institute of Standards and Technology, U.S. Department of Commerce, February 26, 2001. As of February 16, 2015: http://csrc.nist.gov/publications/nistpubs/800-32/sp800-32.pdf

Lajka, Arijeta, "Islamic State Takes a Stab at Legitimacy with Alleged Identification Cards as Forces Lose Ground in Iraq," *Vice News*, April 16, 2015. As of June 25, 2015:
https://news.vice.com/article/islamic-state-takes-a-stab-at-legitimacy-with-alleged-identification-cards-as-forces-lose-ground-in-iraq

Lanxon, Nate, and Adam Satariano, "Hardly Anyone Paying the Hackers? Because Using Bitcoin Is Hard," Bloomberg News, May 15, 2017. As of February 21, 2019:
https://www.bloomberg.com/news/articles/2017-05-15/
hardly-anyone-paying-the-hackers-because-using-bitcoin-is-hard

Lee, Timothy B., "Major Glitch in Bitcoin Network Sparks Sell-Off; Price Temporarily Falls 23%," Ars Technica, March 12, 2013. As of April 16, 2015:
http://arstechnica.com/business/2013/03/
major-glitch-in-bitcoin-network-sparks-sell-off-price-temporarily-falls-23/

Levitt, Matthew, *Hezbollah: The Global Footprint of Lebanon's Party of God*, Washington, D.C.: Georgetown University Press, 2013.

―――, "Hezbollah's Transnational Organized Crime," Washington Institute for Near East Policy, April 21, 2016. As of July 5, 2016:
https://www.washingtoninstitute.org/policy-analysis/view/
hezbollahs-transnational-organized-crime

Lindholm, Danielle Camner, and Celina B. Realuyo, "Threat Finance: A Critical Enabler for Illicit Networks," in Michael Miklaucic and Jacqueline Brewer, eds., *Convergence: Illicit Networks and National Security in the Age of Globalization*, Washington, D.C.: National Defense University Press, April 2013, pp. 111–130.

Lisanti, Dominic, "Do Failed States Really Breed Terrorists? An Examination of Terrorism in Sub-Saharan Africa Comparing Statistical Approaches with a Fuzzy Set Qualitative Comparative Analysis," CAPERS Workshop, New York: New York University, May 14, 2010.

Litecoin, homepage, undated. As of February 24, 2015:
https://litecoin.org/

Liu, Joseph K., Victor K. Wei, and Duncan S. Wong, "Linkable Spontaneous Anonymous Group Signature for Ad Hoc Groups," Sydney, Australia: Information Security and Privacy 9th Australasian Conference, July 13–15, 2004, pp. 325–335. As of February 21, 2019:
https://eprint.iacr.org/2004/027

Mack, Eric, "The Bitcoin Pizza Purchase That's Worth $7 Million Today," *Forbes*, December 23, 2013. As of March 1, 2019:
https://www.forbes.com/sites/ericmack/2013/12/23/
the-bitcoin-pizza-purchase-thats-worth-7-million-today/#587ce9e82509

Maidsafe, homepage, undated. As of on February 24, 2015:
http://maidsafe.net

Mas, Ignacio, and Dan Radcliffe, "Mobile Payments Go Viral: M-PESA in Kenya," World Bank, March 2010. As of February 19, 2015:
http://siteresources.worldbank.org/AFRICAEXT/Resources/258643-1271798012256/M-PESA_Kenya.pdf

Mazacoin, homepage, undated. As of February 24, 2015:
https://mazacoin.org/

McGovern, Julia, "Bitcoin Mining Pool GHash.IO Is Preventing Accumulation of 51% of All Hashing Power," Cex.io blog post, January 9, 2014. As of February 23, 2015:
https://blog.cex.io/news/bitcoin-mining-pool-ghash-io-is-preventing-accumulation-of-51-of-all-hashing-power-14474

McKendry, Ian, "ISIL May Be Using Bitcoin, Fincen's Calvery Says," *American Banker*, November 16, 2015. As of February 19, 2019:
https://www.americanbanker.com/news/isil-may-be-using-bitcoin-fincens-calvery-says

McMillan, Robert, "The Inside Story of Mt. Gox, Bitcoin's $460 Million Disaster," Wired online, March 3, 2014. As of September 29, 2015:
http://www.wired.com/2014/03/bitcoin-exchange

Meiklejohn, Sarah, Marjori Pomarole, Grant Jordan, Kirill Levchenko, Damon McCoy, Geoffrey M. Voelker, and Stefan Savage, "A Fistful of Bitcoins: Characterizing Payments Among Men with No Names," *Proceedings of the 2013 Conference on Internet Measurement (IMC '13)*, October 2013, pp. 127–140.

MEMRI Cyber and Jihad Lab, "Salafi-Jihadis Conduct Online 'Equip Us' Campaign to Raise Funds for Jihad in Gaza," December 16, 2015. As of February 21, 2019:
http://cjlab.memri.org/lab-projects/monitoring-jihadi-and-hacktivist-activity/salafi-jihadis-conduct-online-equip-us-campaign-to-raise-funds-for-jihad-in-gaza/

"Monero.How," homepage, undated. As of January 20, 2018:
https://www.monero.how/

Murphy, Edward V., M. Maureen Murphy, and Michael V. Seitzinger, *Bitcoin: Questions, Answers, and Analysis of Legal Issues*, Washington, D.C.: Congressional Research Service, October 13, 2015.

Nakamoto, Satoshi, "Bitcoin: A Peer-to-Peer Electronic Cash System," self-published paper, 2008. As of February 15, 2015:
https://bitcoin.org/bitcoin.pdf

Nakamura, Yuji, "New Digital Currency Spikes as Drug Dealers Get More Secrecy" Bloomberg News, August 29, 2016. As of February 21, 2019:
http://www.bloomberg.com/news/articles/2016-08-29/new-digital-currency-spikes-after-giving-criminals-more-secrecy

Namecoin, homepage, undated. As of February 24, 2015:
http://namecoin.info/

Narayanan, Arvind, Joseph Bonneau, Edward W. Felten, Andrew Miller, and Steven Goldfeder, *Bitcoin and Cryptocurrency Technologies: A Comprehensive Introduction*, Princeton, N.J.: Princeton University Press, 2016.

Nauert, Heather, "ISIS Parks Its Cash in Bitcoin, Experts Say," Fox News, November 2011.

New Sky Security, "Cryptocurrency Mining Hacks: How Thefts Steal Bitcoin and Ethereum," Medium blog post, April 24, 2018. As of June 15, 2018:
https://blog.newskysecurity.com/cryptocurrency-mining-hacks-how-thefts-steal-bitcoin-and-ethereum-903b215dbbba

Noether, Shen, "Ring Signature Confidential Transactions for Monero," Cryptology ePrint Archive, November 11, 2015. As of February 21, 2019:
https://eprint.iacr.org/2015/1098.pdf

———, "Broken Crypto in Shadowcash," archived shnoe Wordpress blog, February 11, 2016. As of February 21, 2019:
https://web.archive.org/web/20160218042108/https://shnoe.wordpress.com/2016/02/11/de-anonymizing-shadowcash-and-oz-coin/

Nxt Wiki, "Whitepaper:NXT," modified July 13, 2014.

Oftedal, Emilie, *The Financing of Jihadi Terrorist Cells in Europe*, Norway: Forsvarets Forskningsinstitutt, January 6, 2015.

"Omni Layer," homepage, undated. As of January 20, 2018:
http://www.omnilayer.org/

Open Hub, "Bitcoin Project Summary," webpage, undated. As of February 26, 2015:
https://www.openhub.net/p/bitcoin

Parker, Luke, "Bitcoin Stealing Malware Evolves Again," Bravenewcoin.com, February 11, 2016. As of December 29, 2016:
http://bravenewcoin.com/news/bitcoin-stealing-malware-evolves-again/

Perfect Money, homepage, undated. As of April 16, 2015:
https://perfectmoney.is

Persi Paoli, Giacomo, Judith Aldridge, Nathan Ryan, and Richard Warnes, *Behind the Curtain: The Illicit Trade of Firearms, Explosives and Ammunition on the Dark Web*, Santa Monica, Calif.: RAND Corporation, RR-2091-PACCS, 2017. As of March 16, 2018:
https://www.rand.org/pubs/research_reports/RR2091.html

Pfajfar, Damjan, Giovanni Sgro, and Wolf Wagner, "Are Alternative Currencies a Substitute or a Complement to Fiat Money? Evidence from Cross-Country Data," *International Journal of Community Currency Research*, Vol. 16, 2012, pp. 45–56.

Pitta, J., "Requiem for a Bright Idea," *Forbes*, November 1, 1999. As of February 26, 2015:
http://www.forbes.com/forbes/1999/1101/6411390a.html

Pouwelse, Johan, Paweł Garbacki, Dick Epema, and Henk Sips, "The Bittorrent P2P File-Sharing System: Measurements and Analysis," in Miguel Castro, ed., *IPTPS 2005 Proceedings of the Fourth International Conference on Peer-to-Peer Systems*, February 2005, pp. 205–216.

Prisco, Giulio, "An Independent Scotland Powered by Bitcoin?" CryptoCoinNews.com, September 17, 2014. As of February 13, 2015:
https://www.cryptocoinsnews.com/an-independent-scotland-powered-by-bitcoin/

Recorded Future, "How Al-Qaeda Uses Encryption Post-Snowden (Part 1)," self-published paper, May 8, 2014a. As of February 17, 2015:
https://www.recordedfuture.com/al-qaeda-encryption-technology-part-1

———, "How Al-Qaeda Uses Encryption Post-Snowden (Part 2)—New Analysis in Collaboration with ReversingLabs," self-published paper, August 1, 2014b. As of February 17, 2015:
https://www.recordedfuture.com/al-qaeda-encryption-technology-part-2

Reid, Fergal, and Martin Harrigan, "An Analysis of Anonymity in the Bitcoin System," arXiv Physics and Society blog, Cornell University, May 7, 2012. As of February 21, 2019:
https://arxiv.org/abs/1107.4524

Ripple, "FAQ," webpage, undated(a). As of March 5, 2019:
https://ripple.com/FAQ/

———, homepage, undated(b). As of February 24, 2015:
https://ripple.com

Rogoff, Kenneth, "Costs and Benefits to Phasing Out Paper Currency," *NBER Macroeconomics Annual 2014*, Vol. 29, 2015, pp. 445–456.

Rosenberg, Matthew, "U.S. Drops Bombs Not Just on ISIS, but on Its Cash, Too," *New York Times*, January 20, 2016. As of February 20, 2019:
https://www.nytimes.com/2016/01/21/us/politics/us-drops-bombs-not-just-on-isis-but-on-its-cash-too.html

Rotberg, Robert I., "Failed States in a World of Terror," *Foreign Affairs*, July 1, 2002. As of February 21, 2019:
http://www.cfr.org/fragile-or-failed-states/failed-states-world-terror/p4733

Saad, Ghareeb, and Mohamad Amin Hasbini, *The Desert Falcon Targeted Attacks*, Kaspersky Lab, February 17, 2015. As of March 5, 2019:
https://securelist.com/the-desert-falcons-targeted-attacks/68817/

Salt Spring Dollars, homepage, undated. As of February 24, 2015:
http://www.saltspringdollars.com

Samani, Raj, "Cybercrime Exposed: Cybercrime-as-a-Service," corporate white paper, Santa Clara, Calif.: McAfee Labs, 2013a. As of March 5, 2019:
https://www.networksasia.net/article/
cybercrime-exposed-cybercrime-service-1372901941

———, "Digital Laundry: An Analysis of Online Currencies, and Their Use in Cybercrime," corporate white paper, Santa Clara, Calif.: McAfee Labs, 2013b. As of March 5, 2019:
https://gssd.mit.edu/search-gssd/site/
digital-laundry-analysis-online-60692-mon-12-15-2014-1450

Saroiu, Stefan, P. Krishna Gummadi, and Steven D. Gribble, "A Measurement Study of Peer-to-Peer File Sharing Systems," in Martin G. Kienzle and Prashant J. Shenoy, eds., *Proceedings of SPIE: Multimedia Computing and Networking (MMCN) 2002*, Vol. 4673, 2002, pp. 156–170.

Sat, Diana Mergenovna, Grigory Olegovich Krylov, Kirill Evgenyevich Bezverbnyi, Alexander Borisovich Kasatkin, and Ivan Aleksandrovich Kornev, "Investigation of Money Laundering Methods Through Cryptocurrency," *Journal of Theoretical and Applied Information Technology*, Vol. 83, No. 2, 2016, pp. 244–254.

Schneier, Bruce, "Details About Juniper's Firewall Backdoor," Schneier on Security blog, April 19, 2016. As of February 21, 2019:
https://www.schneier.com/blog/archives/2016/04/details_about_j.html

Scotcoin, homepage, undated. As of February 19, 2015:
https://scotcoinproject.com/

Shapiro, Jacob N., "Terrorist Decision-Making: Insights from Economics and Political Science," *Perspectives on Terrorism*, Vol. 6, No. 4–5, 2012.

Square, homepage, undated. As of February 19, 2015:
https://squareup.com

Stalinsky, Steven, "The Cryptocurrency-Terrorism Connection Is Too Big to Ignore," *Washington Post*, December 17, 2018. As of February 21, 2019:
https://www.washingtonpost.com/opinions/
the-cryptocurrency-terrorism-connection-is-too-big-to-ignore/2018/12/17/
69ed6ab4-fe4b-11e8-83c0-b06139e540e5_story.html?utm_term=.53ccb6c24834

Taylor, Adam, "The Islamic State (or Someone Pretending to Be It) Is Trying to Raise Funds Using Bitcoin," *Washington Post*, June 9, 2015. As of March 5, 2019:
https://www.washingtonpost.com/news/worldviews/wp/2015/06/09/the-islamic-state-or-someone-pretending-to-be-it-is-trying-to-raise-funds-using-bitcoin/?utm_term=.775a09d73de7

Taylor, Michael Bedford, "Bitcoin and the Age of Bespoke Silicon," paper presented at the International Conference on Compilers, Architecture, and Synthesis for Embedded Systems (CASES), Montreal, Quebec, September 29–October 4, 2013.

Torpey, Kyle, "Darknet Customers Are Demanding Bitcoin Alternative Monero," *Bitcoin Magazine*, August 26, 2016. As of February 21, 2019:
https://bitcoinmagazine.com/articles/
darknet-customers-are-demanding-bitcoin-alternative-monero-1472243603

Tor Project, "Anonymity Online," webpage, undated(a). As of February 16, 2015:
https://www.torproject.org

———, "Hidden Service Protocol," webpage, undated(b). As of February 16, 2015:
https://www.torproject.org/docs/hidden-services.html.en

———, "Overview," webpage, undated(c). As of February 16, 2015:
https://www.torproject.org/about/overview

———, "Security Advisory Relay Early Traffic," webpage, July 30, 2014a. As of February 16, 2015:
https://blog.torproject.org/blog/
tor-security-advisory-relay-early-traffic-confirmation-attack

———, "Category, Tags, Attacks," webpage, December 19, 2014b. As of February 16, 2015:
https://blog.torproject.org/category/tags/attacks

Totnes Pound, homepage, undated. As of February 24, 2015:
http://www.totnespound.org

Treisman, Daniel, "Russia's 'Ethical Revival': The Separatist Activism of Regional Leaders in a Postcommunist Order," *World Politics*, Vol. 49, No. 2, 1997, pp. 212–249.

U.S. Department of Justice, "Virginia Teen Pleads Guilty to Providing Material Support to ISIL," Washington, D.C.: Office of Public Affairs, June 11, 2015. As of February 21, 2019:
https://www.justice.gov/opa/pr/
virginia-teen-pleads-guilty-providing-material-support-isil

U.S. Department of Justice, U.S. Attorney's Office, Southern District of New York, "Indictment and Supporting Documents: U.S. v. Liberty Reserve et al.," May 28, 2013. As of February 22, 2015:
http://www.justice.gov/usao/nys/pressreleases/May13/
LibertyReserveetalDocuments.php

U.S. House of Representatives, Financial Innovation and Defense Act, H.R. 4752, January 20, 2018. As of January 12, 2018:
https://www.congress.gov/bill/115th-congress/house-bill/4752/
text?q=%7B%22search%22%3A%5B%22H.R.4752%22%5D%7D&r=1

Vandervort, David, Dale Gaucas, and Robert St. Jacques, "Issues in Designing a Bitcoin-Like Community Currency," paper presented at the Second Workshop on Bitcoin Research, San Juan, Puerto Rico, January 30, 2015.

Virga, Joy Marie, "International Criminals and Their Virtual Currencies: The Need for an International Effort in Regulating Virtual Currencies and Combating Cyber Crime," *Brazilian Journal of International Law*, Vol. 12, No. 2, 2015, pp. 512–527.

Wallace, Benjamin, "The Rise and Fall of Bitcoin," *Wired*, November 23, 2011. As of February 21, 2019:
http://www.wired.com/magazine/2011/11/mf_bitcoin

Warren, Jonathan, "Bitmessage: A Peer-to-Peer Message Authentication and Delivery System," self-published paper, November 27, 2012. As of February 23, 2015:
https://bitmessage.org/bitmessage.pdf

Weatherford, Jack McIver, *The History of Money*, New York: Crown Publishers, 1997.

WebMoney Transfer, homepage, undated. As of April 16, 2015:
http://www.wmtransfer.com

Wikipedia, "Ora (Currency)," webpage, April 27, 2015. As of April 21, 2015:
http://en.wikipedia.org/wiki/Ora_%28currency%29

Willett, J. R., *The Second Bitcoin White Paper*, vs. 0.5 (Draft for Public Comment), self-published paper, undated. As of October 1, 2015:
https://sites.google.com/site/2ndbtcwpaper/2ndBitcoinWhitepaper.pdf

Winter, Charlie, and Colin P. Clarke, "Is ISIS Breaking Apart? What Its Media Operations Suggest," *Foreign Affairs*, January 31, 2017. As of February 21, 2019:
https://www.foreignaffairs.com/articles/2017-01-31/isis-breaking-apart

Winter, Philipp, and Stefan Lindskog, "How the Great Firewall of China Is Blocking Tor," paper presented at the Second USENIX Workshop on Free and Open Communication on the Internet (FOCI), Bellevue, Wash., August 2012.

World Bank, "Global Findex Database," 2014. As of June 25, 2015:
http://datatopics.worldbank.org/financialinclusion

Woro Yuniar, Resty, "Bitcoin, PayPal Used to Finance Terrorism, Indonesian Agency Says," *Wall Street Journal*, January 10, 2017. As of February 20, 2019:
https://www.wsj.com/articles/
bitcoin-paypal-used-to-finance-terrorism-indonesian-agency-says-1483964198

Zarate, Juan C., *Treasury's War: The Unleashing of a New Era of Financial Warfare*, New York: PublicAffairs, Perseus Book Group, 2013.

Zerocash Project, homepage, undated. As of February 22, 2015:
http://zerocash-project.org

Zerocoin Project, homepage, undated. As of February 22, 2015:
http://zerocoin.org

Zetter, Kim, "Flame Hijacks Microsoft Update to Spread Malware Disguised as Legit Code," *Wired*, June 4, 2012. As of February 21, 2019:
https://www.wired.com/2012/06/flame-microsoft-certificate/